Lecture Notes in Computer Science   12994

More information about this subseries at https://link.springer.com/bookseries/7408

Chengzhong Xu · Yunni Xia ·
Yuchao Zhang · Liang-Jie Zhang (Eds.)

Web Services – ICWS 2021

28th International Conference
Held as Part of the Services Conference Federation, SCF 2021
Virtual Event, December 10–14, 2021
Proceedings

Springer

Editors
Chengzhong Xu
University of Macau
Macau, China

Yuchao Zhang
Beijing University of Posts and
Telecommunications
Beijing, China

Yunni Xia
Chongqing University
Chongqing, China

Liang-Jie Zhang 🆔
Kingdee International Software Group
Co., Ltd.
Shenzhen, China

ISSN 0302-9743   ISSN 1611-3349 (electronic)
Lecture Notes in Computer Science
ISBN 978-3-030-96139-8   ISBN 978-3-030-96140-4   (eBook)
https://doi.org/10.1007/978-3-030-96140-4

LNCS Sublibrary: SL2 – Programming and Software Engineering

This Springer imprint is published by the registered company Springer Nature Switzerland AG
The registered company address is: Gewerbestrasse 11, 6330 Cham, Switzerland

Preface

The International Conference on Web Services (ICWS) is a prime international forum for both researchers and industry practitioners to exchange the latest fundamental advances in the state of the art and practice of web-based services, identify emerging research topics, and define the future of web-based services. All topics regarding Internet/Web services lifecycle study and management align with the theme of ICWS.

ICWS is a member of Services Conference Federation (SCF). SCF 2021 featured the following 10 collocated service-oriented sister conferences: the International Conference on Web Services (ICWS 2021), the International Conference on Cloud Computing (CLOUD 2021), the International Conference on Services Computing (SCC 2021), the International Conference on Big Data (BigData 2021), the International Conference on AI and Mobile Services (AIMS 2021), the World Congress on Services (SERVICES 2021), the International Conference on Internet of Things (ICIOT 2021), the International Conference on Cognitive Computing (ICCC 2021), the International Conference on Edge Computing (EDGE 2021), and the International Conference on Blockchain (ICBC 2021). As the founding member of SCF, the first International Conference on Web Services (ICWS) was held in June 2003 in Las Vegas, USA.

This volume presents the accepted papers for ICWS 2021, held virtually over the Internet during December 10–14, 2021. For this conference, each paper was reviewed by three independent members of the international Program Committee. After carefully evaluating their originality and quality, we accepted seven papers.

We are pleased to thank the authors whose submissions and participation made this conference possible. We also want to express our thanks to the Organizing Committee and Program Committee members for their dedication in helping to organize the conference and reviewing the submissions. We owe special thanks to the keynote speakers for their impressive speeches.

Finally, we would like to thank operations committee members Sheng He and Yishuang Ning for their excellent work in organizing this conference. We look forward to your future contributions as volunteers, authors, and conference participants for the fast-growing worldwide services innovations community.

December 2021

Chengzhong Xu
Yunni Xia
Yuchao Zhang
Liang-Jie Zhang

Organization

General Chairs

Hai Jin   Huazhong University of Science and Technology, China

Xiaoqing Liu   Southern Illinois University, USA

Program Chairs

Chengzhong Xu   University of Macau, China

Yunni Xia   Chongqing University, China

Yuchao Zhang   Beijing University of Posts and Telecommunications, China

Services Conference Federation (SCF 2021)

General Chairs

Wu Chou   Essenlix Corporation, USA

Calton Pu (Co-chair)   Georgia Tech, USA

Dimitrios Georgakopoulos   Swinburne University of Technology, Australia

Program Chairs

Liang-Jie Zhang   Kingdee International Software Group Co., Ltd., China

Ali Arsanjani   Amazon Web Services, USA

CFO

Min Luo   Georgia Tech, USA

Industry Track Chairs

Awel Dico   Etihad Airways, UAE

Rajesh Subramanyan   Amazon Web Services, USA

Siva Kantamneni   Deloitte Consulting, USA

Industry Exhibit and International Affairs Chair

Zhixiong Chen   Mercy College, USA

Operations Committee

Jing Zeng   China Gridcom Co., Ltd., China
Yishuang Ning   Tsinghua University, China
Sheng He   Tsinghua University, China

Steering Committee

Calton Pu (Co-chair)   Georgia Tech, USA
Liang-Jie Zhang (Co-chair)   Kingdee International Software Group Co., Ltd., China

ICWS 2021 Program Committee

Ismailcem Arpinar   University of Georgia, USA
Yacine Atif   University of Skovde, Sweden
Amin Beheshti   Macquarie University, Australia
Ladjel Bellatreche   LISI/ENSMA University of Poitiers, France
Salima Benbernou   Université de Paris, France
Abdelghani Benharref   University of Wollongong, Australia
Nizar Bouguila   Concordia University, Canada
Bo Cheng   Beijing University of Posts and Telecommunications,
                             China
Hadeel El-Kassabi   United Arab Emirates University, UAE
Keke Gai   Beijing Institute of Technology, China
Abdul Kadhim Hayawi   Zayed University, UAE
Loïc Hélouët   Inria, France
Heba Ismail   United Arab Emirates University, UAE
Adel Khelifi   Abu Dhabi University, UAE
Hyuk-Yoon Kwon   Seoul National University of Science and Technology,
                             South Korea
Bing Li   Wuhan University, China
Zakaria Maamar   Zayed University, UAE
Sujith Mathew   Zayed University, UAE
Rabeb Mizouni   Khalifa University, UAE
Roy Oberhauser   Aalen University, Germany
Hadi Otrok   Khalifa University, UAE
Sofia Ouhbi   United Arab Emirates University, UAE
Ali Ouni   University of Quebec, Canada
Dhaval Patel   IBM T. J. Watson Research Center, USA
Young-Kyoon Suh   Kyungpook National University, South Korea
Ikbal Taleb   Zayed University, UAE
Liqiang Wang   University of Central Florida, USA

Songmei Yu   Felician University, USA
Rui Zhang   Institute of Information Engineering, Chinese Academy
                               of Sciences, China
Yuchao Zhang   Beijing University of Posts and Telecommunications,
                               China

Conference Sponsor – Services Society

The Services Society (S2) is a non-profit professional organization that has been created to promote worldwide research and technical collaboration in services innovations among academia and industrial professionals. Its members are volunteers from industry and academia with common interests. S2 is registered in the USA as a "501(c) organization", which means that it is an American tax-exempt nonprofit organization. S2 collaborates with other professional organizations to sponsor or co-sponsor conferences and to promote an effective services curriculum in colleges and universities. The S2 initiates and promotes a "Services University" program worldwide to bridge the gap between industrial needs and university instruction.

The Services Sector has account for 79.5% of the GDP of United States in 2016. The world's most services oriented economy, with services sectors accounting for more than 90% of GDP. The Services Society has formed 10 Special Interest Groups (SIGs) to support technology and domain specific professional activities.

- Special Interest Group on Web Services (SIG-WS)
- Special Interest Group on Services Computing (SIG-SC)
- Special Interest Group on Services Industry (SIG-SI)
- Special Interest Group on Big Data (SIG-BD)
- Special Interest Group on Cloud Computing (SIG-CLOUD)
- Special Interest Group on Artificial Intelligence (SIG-AI)
- Special Interest Group on Edge Computing (SIG-EC)
- Special Interest Group on Cognitive Computing (SIG-CC)
- Special Interest Group on Blockchain (SIG-BC)
- Special Interest Group on Internet of Things (SIG-IOT)

About Services Conference Federation (SCF)

As the founding member of the Services Conference Federation (SCF), the first International Conference on Web Services (ICWS) was held in June 2003 in Las Vegas, USA. Meanwhile, the First International Conference on Web Services - Europe 2003 (ICWS-Europe'03) was held in Germany in Oct, 2003. ICWS-Europe'03 is an extended event of the 2003 International Conference on Web Services (ICWS 2003) in Europe. In 2004, ICWS-Europe was changed to the European Conference on Web Services (ECOWS), which was held at Erfurt, Germany. SCF 2020 was held successfully. To celebrate its 19-year-old birthday, SCF 2021 was held virtually over the Internet on December 10–14, 2021.

In the past 18 years, ICWS community has been expanded from Web engineering innovations to scientific research for the whole services industry. The service delivery platforms have been expanded to mobile platforms, Internet of Things, cloud computing, and edge computing. The services ecosystem is gradually enabled, value added, and intelligence embedded through enabling technologies such as big data, artificial intelligence, and cognitive computing. In the coming years, all the transactions with multiple parties involved will be transformed to blockchain.

Based on the technology trends and best practices in the field, SCF will continue serving as the conference umbrella's code name for all services-related conferences. SCF 2021 defines the future of New ABCDE (AI, Blockchain, Cloud, big Data, Everything is connected), which enable IOT and enter the 5G for Services Era. SCF 2021's 10 co-located theme topic conferences all center around "services", while each focusing on exploring different themes (web-based services, cloud-based services, Big Data-based services, services innovation lifecycle, AI-driven ubiquitous services, blockchain driven trust service-ecosystems, industry-specific services and applications, and emerging service-oriented technologies). SCF includes 10 service-oriented conferences: ICWS, CLOUD, SCC, BigData Congress, AIMS, SERVICES, ICIOT, EDGE, ICCC and ICBC. The SCF 2021 members are listed as follows:

[1] The 2021 International Conference on Web Services (ICWS 2021, http://icws. org/) is the flagship theme-topic conference for Web-based services, featuring Web services modeling, development, publishing, discovery, composition, testing, adaptation, delivery, as well as the latest API standards.

[2] The 2021 International Conference on Cloud Computing (CLOUD 2021, http:// thecloudcomputing.org/) is the flagship theme-topic conference for modeling, developing, publishing, monitoring, managing, delivering XaaS (everything as a service) in the context of various types of cloud environments.

[3] The 2021 International Conference on Big Data (BigData 2021, http:// bigdatacongress.org/) is the emerging theme-topic conference for the scientific and engineering innovations of big data.

[4] The 2021 International Conference on Services Computing (SCC 2021, http:// thescc.org/) is the flagship theme-topic conference for services innovation

lifecycle that includes enterprise modeling, business consulting, solution creation, services orchestration, services optimization, services management, services marketing, business process integration and management.

[5] The 2021 International Conference on AI & Mobile Services (AIMS 2021, http://ai1000.org/) is the emerging theme-topic conference for the science and technology of artificial intelligence, and the development, publication, discovery, orchestration, invocation, testing, delivery, and certification of AI-enabled services and mobile applications.

[6] The 2021 World Congress on Services (SERVICES 2021, http://servicescongress.org/) puts its focus on emerging service-oriented technologies and the industry-specific services and solutions.

[7] The 2021 International Conference on Cognitive Computing (ICCC 2021, http://thecognitivecomputing.org/) puts its focus on the Sensing Intelligence (SI) as a Service (SIaaS) that makes system listen, speak, see, smell, taste, understand, interact, and walk in the context of scientific research and engineering solutions.

[8] The 2021 International Conference on Internet of Things (ICIOT 2021, http://iciot.org/) puts its focus on the creation of Internet of Things technologies and development of IOT services.

[9] The 2021 International Conference on Edge Computing (EDGE 2021, http://theedgecomputing.org/) puts its focus on the state of the art and practice of edge computing including but not limited to localized resource sharing, connections with the cloud, and 5G devices and applications.

[10] The 2021 International Conference on Blockchain (ICBC 2021, http://blockchain1000.org/) concentrates on blockchain-based services and enabling technologies.

Some highlights of SCF 2021 are shown below:

– **Bigger Platform:** The 10 collocated conferences (SCF 2021) get sponsorship from the Services Society which is the world-leading not-for-profits organization (501 c(3)) dedicated for serving more than 30,000 worldwide Services Computing researchers and practitioners. Bigger platform means bigger opportunities to all volunteers, authors and participants. Meanwhile, Springer provides sponsorship to best paper awards and other professional activities. All the 10 conference proceedings of SCF 2021 have been published by Springer and indexed in ISI Conference Proceedings Citation Index (included in Web of Science), Engineering Index EI (Compendex and Inspec databases), DBLP, Google Scholar, IO-Port, MathSciNet, Scopus, and ZBlMath.
– **Brighter Future:** While celebrating 2021 version of ICWS, SCF 2021 highlights the Fourth International Conference on Blockchain (ICBC 2021) to build the fundamental infrastructure for enabling secure and trusted services ecosystems. It will also lead our community members to create their own brighter future.
– **Better Model:** SCF 2021 continues to leverage the invented Conference Blockchain Model (CBM) to innovate the organizing practices for all the 10 theme conferences.

Contents

Cloud-WSDL: Making WSDL Suitable for Cloud Computing

Souad Ghazouani[1], Anis Tissaoui[2(✉)], and Richard Chbeir[3]

[1] LISI Laboratory of Computer Science for Industrial Systems, Carthage University, Tunis, Tunisia
[2] VPNC Lab., FSJEG, University of Jendouba, Avenue Union Maghreb Arabe, 8189 Jendouba, Tunisia
anis.tissaoui@fsjegj.rnu.tn
[3] Univ. Pau and Pays Adour, E2S UPPA, LIUPPA, 64600 Anglet, France
rchbeir@acm.org

Abstract. Several approaches have been proposed to describe services in a rich and generic manner (such as WSDL, OWL-S, WSMO, and SAWSDL). However, current approaches remain inappropriate for cloud computing since: 1) they lack in a way or another semantic or business aspect, 2) they cannot fully cope with non-functional properties, 3) they are unable to cover all kinds of services (such as SaaS, PaaS, IaaS). Despite the existence of several attempts which have tried to extent existing studies, the problem remains open. In this paper, we propose Cloud-WSDL, a new description model aligned with WSDL language, the most popular language, to make it more suitable for describing cloud services. The idea is to enhance WSDL description with new functional, non-functional and cloud features so to cope with many aspects (technical, operational, business, semantic and contextual). The proposed extension ensures a high interoperability between services belonging to multiple heterogeneous clouds, and supports all the kinds of cloud services (SaaS, PaaS, and IaaS). To do that, we rely on MDA principle to extent WSDL metamodel through several metamodel transformation. The extension process begins by transforming WSDL metamodel into Cloud-WSDL metamodel, thus we obtain a syntactic Cloud-WSDL extension. After that, as a second step, the produced model is transformed into an OWL-S ontology to offer a semantic Cloud-WSDL extension.

Keywords: Cloud service · Generic cloud service description · WSDL · OWL-S ontology · Cloud computing

1 Introduction

Service description consists in defining an interface describing the operations carried out by the service and linking each operation to its realization. It ensures the communication between the consumer and the provider. The service description should be defined in a readable and interpretable language for both humans and

© Springer Nature Switzerland AG 2022
C. Xu et al. (Eds.): ICWS 2021, LNCS 12994, pp. 1–14, 2022.
https://doi.org/10.1007/978-3-030-96140-4_1

machines in order to enhance the service discovery and composition. Although commonly adopted, *Web Services Description Language* or WSDL cannot ensure this since it is syntactic oriented. Semantic oriented service description is needed to ensure that, where the capabilities of each service are associated with semantic concepts to enhance both discovery and selection processes.

In this context, several semantic oriented approaches [1–8] have been proposed in the literature to offer a detailed service description and overcome WSDL limitations. However, the major limitations of these approaches are related to the fact that they don't cover the semantic level, the non-functional properties and the contextual information.

In cloud computing, most of services are described as Web services using different languages such as WSDL, OWL-S, and WSMO. However, the existing languages are arisen to the Web and not for cloud computing domain. That is why, several attempts [11–14] have emerged recently to provide a richer service description so to support SaaS, PaaS, and IaaS services.

The proposed approaches to describe cloud services have, also, some limitations. So, they are intended to be used for specific tasks only (service description task, service discovery task, service composition task, etc.). Also, they do not cover all cloud concepts (pricing, legal, SLA, etc.). Besides, they focus on specifying some dedicated aspects (for example the technical aspect only) and they fail to cover all aspects (technical, operational, business, and semantic). For instance, WSDL covers only technical aspect and does not cover business and semantic ones.

Furthermore, service providers have used various techniques such as models [10, 21], taxonomy [22], languages [13, 23–25], ontologies [26–28], and template [29, 30] to describe their cloud services. The diversity of techniques leads to the vendor lock-in problem and thus the interoperability issue.

Several challenges are to be met when describing cloud services, mainly:

- How to represent the functional properties of cloud services?
- How to specify the non-functional properties of cloud services?
- How to specify the cloud characteristics?
- How to describe all cloud services (SaaS, PaaS, IaaS)? and

To do that, we follow an extension process including two steps: the first one is responsible for transforming WSDL metamodel to Cloud-WSDL metamodel, which helps to obtain a syntactic Cloud-WSDL extension. The second step helps to translate the resulting extension to a semantic Cloud-WSDL extension.

So, Cloud-WSDL is a description devoted to cloud computing and derived from the famous language WSDL. It makes WSDL able to cover several aspects: technical (functional properties), operational (functional properties), business (non-functional properties) and semantic. Besides, Cloud-WSDL takes into account the contextual aspect to support the context adaptation.

The rest of this paper is structured as follows. In Sect. 2, we give an overview of WSDL and its extensions. In Sect. 3, we explain the requirements for a generic cloud service description. Section 4 introduces the extension process that we will follow to enhance WSDL. Section 5 presents the new extension of WSDL metamodel named Cloud-WSDL. We describe in Sect. 6, the tools used to manipulate the new WSDL extension and we compare this latter with other languages. Section 7 concludes this study and provides several perspectives.

2   Background and Related Work

In this section, we give an overview on WSDL and present the main alternatives for its extensions.

2.1   WSDL

WSDL language is a W3C standard that describes a service through an interface presenting a set of operations and their respective input and output parameters in the form of an XML document. The WSDL interface describes the functionality accomplished by the service (what the service does), but it does not describe how to accomplish this functionality (how the service does it). As shown in Fig. 1, the WSDL document contains 5 kinds of XML elements: *<typoo>*, *<messuye>*, *<pot lType>*, *<binding>* and *<service>*.

The information contained in WSDL essentially corresponds to the description of the functional profile of the service. With WSDL, the client can invoke the service by referring to the information in its WSDL file, providing information on its abstract description (available methods, input and output parameters, etc.) and its concrete description (description of communication protocols, service access points, etc.). The main problem with WSDL is its limitation to characterize the semantics of the functionality accomplished by the service. To overcome the lack of semantics of WSDL, several approaches have been proposed to add a layer on top of WSDL supplementing the syntactic description by semantic precision. We will detail, later, the best known approaches and show their limitations.

2.2   Semantic Extensions

To overcome the semantic limitation of WSDL, several research studies have been provided in the literature.

On one hand, some of them adopted *semantic annotations*. These consist in enriching and completing the description of a service by establishing correspondences between elements of the WSDL description and concepts of a set of reference ontologies (OWL-S [19], WSMO [20], etc.). In [1], the authors have proposed WSDL-S. It consists in annotating the WSDL specification by ontological concepts. Its meta-model allows the addition of 3 elements: *<category>*, *<precondition>*, *<effect>* and 2 attributes *modelReference* and *schemaMapping*. In [2], the authors have proposed SAWSDL, which is also an extension of WSDL to cover the semantic aspect. The specification annotates a WSDL 2.0 document with the following attributes: *modelReference, liftingSchemaMapping,* and *loweringSchemaMapping*. In particular, it annotates the elements: *operations, input, output, type schemas,* and *interfaces*.

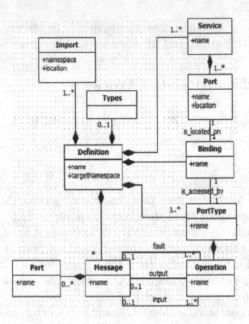

Fig. 1. Metamodel of WSDL

On the other hand, several studies tempted to rely on OWL-S. The authors of [3] have converted WSDL to OWL-S. They have proposed a service annotation framework. The idea is to annotate WSDL service descriptions with metadata from OWL-S ontology. The solution starts by aligning concepts of WSDL with OWL. It converts each of them to a common representation (called schema Graph). After the schema graphs are created, the matching algorithms are executed on the graphs to determine similarities. So, once the concepts of the schema graph are matched, the concept having the highest matching score is chosen. Likewise for the work presented in [15]. Other researchers aimed at proposing an automatic mapping of WSDL to OWL-S such as [7,8,18]. In [7], Paolucci et al. have proposed a tool called WSDL2OWL-S, which allows a transition between WSDL and OWL-S. In this attempt, all XSD complex types of WSDL are converted to generate concepts and properties for each type. In this approach, the conversion of XSD types to concepts is done without any relationships between these concepts. This manner of conversion leads to use a lot of concepts and missing semantic web meaning. Another interesting work is presented in [8] where a mapping tool called ASSAM (*Automated Semantic Service Annotation with Machine Learning*) is proposed. ASSAM helps to convert the WSDL file into OWL-S file. It suffers from some limitations: ASSAM cannot provide an organization for the used ontologies, which provides a great number of returned concepts. The list of concepts is found based on the text search and not on the meaning. Also, the concepts provided to users are not ranked by importance. Sagayara et al. [18] have worked on the automatic transformation of complex type WSDL to OWL-S. They have proposed an WO framework which helps to extract the elements from WSDL document and place them, by using OWL-parser, in OWL-S. However, the proposed framework does not modify the concepts after their conversion.

2.3 Non-functional Properties Extensions

Other attempts to enrich WSDL files not only by considering the semantic level in the description of services but also by taking into account the non-functional aspect, like WS-Policy standard [4]. In [5], D'Ambrogio et al. have proposed an extension called P-WSDL (*Performance-enabled WSDL*) which enriches WSDL with several performance properties of Web services. They have followed MDA principle and proposed a metamodel transformation. El Bitar et al. [6] have proposed a semantic description model aligned with standards for the automatic discovery of Web services. They rely on WSDL 2.0 standard and WS-Policy. Also, the work of [16] has proposed an extension, called Q-WSDL, to describe QoS characteristics of a Web service. The authors have followed the principle of MDA for Q-WSDL according to a meta-model transformation. Chabeb et al. [17] have proposed YASA4WSDL (*Yet Another Semantic Annotation for WSDL*) which is an extension of SAWSDL that uses two types of ontologies: (i) *Technical Ontology* which contains concepts defining semantics of services, their QoS.; and, (ii) *Domain Ontology* which contains the concepts defining the semantics of the business domain. However, these approaches have addressed, most of the time, some non-functional properties namely response time, availability, cost and they dismiss the other ones (reputations, risk evaluation, actors, usage license, etc.) which help users to select the suitable service.

2.4 Discussion

As mentioned previously, various extensions of WSDL have been proposed. As depicted in Table 1, most of them have tried to enhance the description from the technical and operational aspects (functional properties) [1–3,5–8,15–18]. While, others have added the non-functional properties [4–6,16,17] and the semantic aspect [1–3,6–8,15,17,18]. However, all these approaches are still inappropriate to cloud computing domain. Indeed, they don't cover cloud characteristis such as: delivery model (SaaS, PaaS, IaaS), deployment model (public, private, hybrid, and community), cloud provider, used resources (RAM size, CPU brand, virtual machine type, etc.), etc. Besides, they don't take into account the contextual information.

Therefore, we aim to enhance WSDL in order to propose a new service description suitable for cloud computing and which is able to support technical, operational, business, semantic and contextual aspects.

Table 1. Comparison between studied approaches.

Approaches	(1)	(2)	(3)	(4)	(5)
[1]	✓			✓	
[2]	✓			✓	
[3]	✓			✓	
[4]		✓			
[5]	✓	✓			
[6]	✓	✓		✓	
[7]	✓			✓	
[8]	✓			✓	
[15]	✓			✓	
[16]	✓	✓			
[17]	✓	✓		✓	
[18]	✓			✓	

(1) Functional properties/(2) Non-functional properties/(3) Cloud characteristics/(4) Semantic aspect/(5) Contextual information

3 Requirements for Cloud Services

Based on the literature [9, 10, 13, 32, 33], we present, in this section, the requirements that should be taken into account to define a generic cloud service description.

R1. Supporting all service delivery models
Cloud services are deployed in three layers (SaaS, PaaS, IaaS). Each type of services has its own characteristics. For that, cloud service description should be generic and describe all types of cloud services.

R2: Supporting all service deployment models
Cloud services are deployed based on different deployment models (public, private, community, and hybrid). Therefore, the service description should describe the knowledge about these deployment models.

R3: Supporting semantic aspect
Semantic aspect helps to enhance the result of service discovery and composition, and thus, it ensures a better result of returned services that satisfy the user needs.

R4: Measurement of service attributes
Evaluation mechanisms help cloud consumers, particularly, the non-technician to choose and select services. Also, service evaluations help service provider to compare its services to other available ones in the marketplace. Besides, they are used for detecting the SLA violations.

R5: Describing different actors
Cloud Computing includes five actors: consumer, provider, broker, auditor, and carrier [13]. So, cloud service description should describe these different actors, their relations and their interactions with their services.

R6: Defining a dynamic actor profile
Consumers have various levels of needs, preferences and skills, which are different from one consumer to another. Each actor has a profile describing him. This latter can be static or dynamic. *Static profile* presents information defined once for all such as consumer name, birth date, etc. However, a *dynamic profile* contains a customized information such as objectives, preferences/desires, skills, constraints, etc. This dynamic profile enhances the service discovery through the selection of the best services that meet consumer requests.

R7: Adaptation of context changes
Service exists in a dynamic environment which may be changed due to various factors such as: service failure, degradation of service quality, change of user needs, or unavailability of services due to a network problem. These external factors can be triggered in unforeseen manner. It is necessary to propose a service description supporting the dynamic changes in the environment.

R8: Well defining environment constraints
Cloud service exists in a variable environment. Its usage is limited by several environmental constraints, which can be time or space constraints. For example, a consumer wants to use cloud services only deployed in the UK. So, he must put constraint on the wanted location.

R9: Well defining SLA between Cloud layers
After selecting services, it is necessary to define different contract elements (provided service definition, guaranties, and penalties). SLA penalty clauses are triggered and executed in the event of a violation happened. Service description model should: (i) well define SLA contract; (ii) well describe penalties; and, (iii) well define a SLA contract between different Cloud layers (SaaS, PaaS, and IaaS).

R10: Supporting service reusability via the service composition
In order to avoid development issues and gain time, reusing and composing existing services become the most useful solution. In cloud computing, *broker* is an entity responsible for managing the service composition. So, cloud service description should allow the service composition, and thus, the service reusability.

We aim, in this work, to enhance WSDL by taking into account these requirements.

4 Transformation Process

In this paper, we adopt MDA (*Model Driven Architecture*) [31] to obtain a new extension of WSDL destined to cloud computing domain. According to MDA, each model is an instance of a MOF metamodel which is, in its turn, an instance of a MOF meta-metamodel.

MOF (*Meta Object Facility*) is the standard of OMG (*Object Management Group*) used to specify metamodels or models in the description of other models.

XML schemas are obtained from MOF metamodels and vice-versa by using XMI (*XML Metadata Interchange*) specification.

WSDL description is an XML document that is obtained by using a WSDL XML Schema. Briefly, an XML document is an instance of an XML Schema, in the same way, a model is an instance of a metamodel. In our work, we will represent WSDL in the form of a metamodel.

As depicted in Fig. 2, our approach is carried out into two steps:

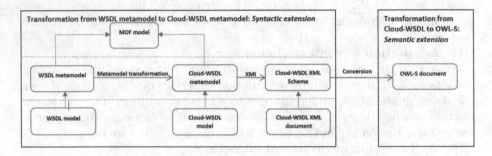

Fig. 2. Transformation from WSDL to semantic Cloud-WSDL extension.

Step 1: Syntactic Cloud-WSDL extension
In this step, we aim to propose a new extension of WSDL metamodel called Cloud-WSDL metamodel. First, the WSDL metamodel is extended by the application of a metamodel transformation which maps WSDL metamodel to Cloud-WSDL metamodel. After that, the Cloud-WSDL metamodel is serialized to Cloud-WSDL XML schema by using XMI rules. The obtained schema is used to produce our model (Cloud-WSDL XML document).

Step 2: Semantic Cloud-WSDL extension
In this step, we aim to add semantic aspect to the new extension, which is a syntactic description (Cloud-WSDL). To do that, we aim to translate WSDL document to OWL-S document based on the mapping between XML document and OWL document, since WSDL document is described by XML and OWL-S document is described by OWL. The mapping between these two documents is done automatically. This step helps to generate an ontology that describes cloud computing domain.

5   Metamodel of Cloud-WSDL

In this section, we will present Cloud-WSDL metamodel, a new semantic extension of WSDL, which is destined to cloud computing domain.

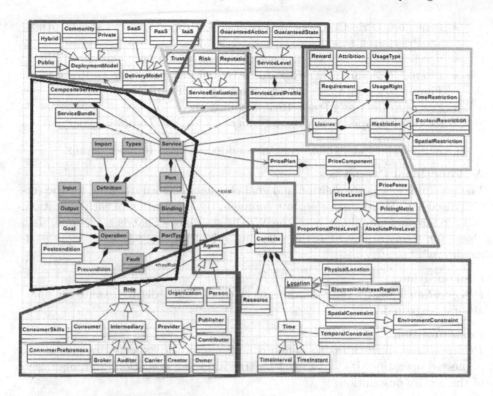

Fig. 3. New metamodel of WSDL after enhancement. (Color figure online)

Figure 3 shows the metamodel of WSDL after extension where all the important properties have been added: actors (blue color), contextual information (pink color), pricing information (green color), legal aspect (orange color), SLA (purple color), cloud-specific information (delivery models (red color), deployment models (red color), service evaluation (yellow color), etc.). All these properties have been inspired from several research works [9–14,21,22,26,27,29] addressing the cloud service description.

As depicted in Fig. 3, we can categorize the new added elements to WSDL metamodel into:

– **Functional properties:** *Service, Definition, Import, Types, Operation, Input, Output, Precondition, Postconditon, Goal, Port, Binding, PortType, Fault, CompositeService, ServiceBundle, Resource. Resource* is considered as a functional property. For example, a user looks for an IaaS service which has storage size equal to "500 GB", RAM equal to "4 GB" and CPU kind is "Intel Xeon".
– **Non-functional properties:**
  • *DeploymentModel* (Public, Private, Hybrid, Community),
  • *DeliveryModel* (SaaS, PaaS, IaaS),

- *PricePlan* (PriceComponent, PriceLevel, ProportionalPriceLevel, AbsolutePriceLevel, PriceFence, PriceMetric),
- *ServiceLevelProfile* (ServiceLevel, GuaranteedAction, GuaranteedState),
- *License* (Requirement, Reward, Attribution, UsageRight, Restriction, TimeRestriction, ContentRestriction, SpatialRestiction),
- *ServiceEvaluation* (Trust, Risk, Reputation),
- **Contextual properties:** *Context, Agent, Resource, Location, Time, etc.*

In the following, we explain each new added element in more details.

A. Functional Properties

The precondition, postcondition and goal elements deemed essential for the service discovery. These three elements complete the description of each operation, while remaining compliant with the WSDL standard. That is why, we add to *Operation* element of WSDL the following sub-elements "*precondition*", "*postcondition*", "*Goal*".

Precondition

Precondition indicates the conditions to be checked in order to execute the operation as expected.

Postcondition

Postcondition allows users to define conditions on the expected results of the requested operation. Its value must be true after the execution of an operation of the service description.

Goal

Goal represents the consumer purpose which enhances the discovery process to find the appropriate service whenever two services have the same inputs and outputs.

B. Non-functional Properties

Since WSDL cannot describe the non-functional properties (price, evaluation, legal aspect, SLA, etc.), we added to WSDL metamodel information about consumption pricing, legal aspect, SLA, reputation, trust, risk, etc. The new information enhances the service discovery process, and thus, meets the user request easily. All these properties are explained in a detailed manner in our previous work [9].

Pricing

PricePlan includes one or more *PriceComponent* associated with different capabilities related to various pricing aspects. *PriceComponent* has monetary value specified via *PriceLevel* which can be fixed per measure (*AbsolutePriceLevel*) or proportional to a some base (*RelativePriceLevel*). *PriceLevel* has *PriceMetric* as a measurement on which pricing is defined. The dynamic variations of Pricing (such as rewards statutes of consumer, bundled deals, and other accepted negotiations with consumer) are supported through *PriceFence*.

Service Evaluation

ServiceEvaluation includes *Reputation*, *Trust* and *Risk*. *Reputation* helps to measure the reputation after service usage from the feedback of users. *Risk* helps to measure the risk produced by the service.

Legal

Each service should be licensed (*License*). The license includes *Usage-Right* which is composed of *UsageType*. This latter puts a well-defined manner of how to use a service (such as the right to distribute). All these properties help users to easily select the suitable services.

C. Contextual Information

A service exists in a context (*Context*). For that, a connection between *Service* and *Context* should be established. However, the context includes *services, agents, resources, location*, and *time*.

Resource concept represents different real-world objects types such as application, system, tool used to perform a service. *Location* covers both physical and virtual addresses (for example, a location of service availability or a valid area for a specific price). *Time* provides means to express (for example, a service availability or a period of prices validity, etc.). The precision of time of service usage or the service location helps to precise the research space of services. Thus, we can say that the contextual information enhances the result of the service discovery.

WSDL is poor from information about context. Therefore, we add these missing information to WSDL metamodel in a detailed manner as depicted in Fig. 3.

6   Experiments and Evaluation

To manipulate and edit Cloud-WSDL descriptions, we have used EMF (*Eclipse Modelling Framework Project*) [34]. Also, we have added OWL-S API to Eclipse to manage OWL-S and thus to generate OWL-S descriptions from Cloud-WSDL descriptions. The prototype aims, in the first step, to transform WSDL document to Cloud-WSDL document. The transformation result is stored in an XML file. Afterwards, the obtained document is transformed to OWL description (OWL-S ontology).

Based on the literature, we present in Table 2 a comparison between WSDL, OWL-S, WSMO and our proposed extension Cloud-WSDL according to some criteria (functional properties, non-functional properties, semantic aspect, cloud computing, contextual information, etc.).

We notice that Cloud-WSDL can handle in a better way cloud computing. Unlike the other existing descriptions languages (WSDL, OWL-S and WSMO), it takes into consideration several criteria: (i) functional and non-functional properties such as input, output, precondition, postcondition, effect, assumption, actor; (iii) cloud characteristics (deployment model, delivery model, SLA, license, etc.); (iii) semantic aspect; and, (iv) contextual aspect.

Table 2. Comparison between WSDL, OWL-S, WSMO and Cloud-WSDL.

Criteria	WSDL	OWL-S	WSMO	Cloud-WSDL
(1)	Operation	AtomicProcess	Choreogaphy	Function
	Input	Input		InputParameter
	Output	Output		OutputParameter
		Precondition	Precondition	Precondition
			PostCondition	PostCondition
		Result	Effect	Effect
			Assumption	Assumption
		CompositeService	Orchestration	CompositeService
	Fault	Fault		Fault
(2)		Participant, Provider, Consumer, physicalAddress, email, phone, fax, WebURL	Owner, Creator	Provider, Creator, Owner, Consumer, Role, Agent, Person, Organization, PricePlan, ServiceLevelProfile, License, ServiceEvaluation
(3)				*Resource* (OS, CPU, RAM, Storage), *DeploymentModel* (Public, Private, Hybrid, Community), *DeliveryModel* (SaaS, PaaS, IaaS)
(4)				Context, Agent, Resource, Location, Time, etc.
(5)		✓	✓	✓

(1) Functional properties/(2) Non-functional properties/(3) Cloud characteristics/(4) Contextual information/(5) Semantic aspect

7   Conclusion

WSDL is the popular language used to describe Web services. However, it covers only the functional properties of services and lacks semantic aspect. Also, it can't cover the non-functional properties and the contextual information. Furthermore, WSDL isn't dedicated to cloud computing not support its characteristics. To overcome these shortages, we enhance, in this paper, WSDL with several properties. Our proposal is obtained according to MDA principle after two transformation steps starting with a transformation from WSDL metamodel to Cloud-WSDL metamodel and, then, a transformation from Cloud-WSDL metamodel to an OWL-S ontology. The new extension supports functional and non-functional properties, contextual information, cloud characteristics and the semantic aspect. The proposed WSDL extension ensures a high interoperability and improves the result of service discovery.

In our future work, we aim to propose two new extensions by enhancing OWL-S and WSMO and make them appropriate for cloud computing domain.

References

1. Akkiraju, R., Farrell, J., Miller, J.: Web service semantics - WSDL-S. A joint UGA-IBM Technical Note, version 1.0, Technical report, UGA-IBM, April 2005
2. Farrell, J., Lausen, H.: Semantic annotations for WSDL and XML schema. W3C recommendation (2007). http://www.w3.org/TR/sawsdl/
3. Patil, A.A., Oundhakar, S.A., Sheth, A.P.: METEOR-S web service annotation framework. In: 13th International Conference on World Wide Web, pp. 553–562 (2004)
4. Vedamuthu, A., Orchard, D., Hirsch, F.: Web services policy 1.5 - framework. W3C recommendation (2007). http://www.w3.org/TR/ws-policy/
5. D'Ambrogio, A.: A WSDL extension for performance-enabled description of web services. In: Yolum, I., Güngör, T., Gürgen, F., Özturan, C. (eds.) ISCIS 2005. LNCS, vol. 3733, pp. 371–381. Springer, Heidelberg (2005). https://doi.org/10.1007/11569596_40
6. El Bitar, I., Belouadha, F.-Z., Roudies, O.: Towards a semantic description model aligned with W3C standards for WS automatic discovery. In: 2014 International Conference on Multimedia Computing and Systems (ICMCS), 14–16 April 2014. IEEE, Marrakech (2014)
7. Paolucci, M., Srinivasan, N., Sycara, K.: Towards a semantic choreography of Web services: from WSDL to DAML-S. In: The International Conference on Web Services, pp. 22–26. IEEE (2003)
8. Heß, A., Johnston, E., Kushmerick, N.: ASSAM: a tool for semi-automatically annotating semantic web services. In: The 12th International Conference of Web Technologies, pp. 470–475 (2008)
9. Ghazouani, S., Slimani, Y.: Towards a standardized Cloud service description based on USDL. J. Syst. Softw. 132, 1–20 (2017)
10. Barros, A., Oberle, D.: Handbook of Service Description: USDL and Its Methods. Springer, New York (2012). https://doi.org/10.1007/978-1-4614-1864-1
11. Liu, D., Zic, J.: Cloud#: a specification language for modeling Cloud. In: 2011 IEEE International Conference on Cloud Computing (CLOUD), 4–9 July 2011, pp. 533–540. IEEE, Washington, DC (2011)
12. Hamdaqa, M., Livogiannis, T., Tahvildari, L.: A reference model for developing cloud applications. In: 1st International Conference on Cloud Computing and Services Science, pp. 98–103. SciTePress (2011)
13. Sun, L., Ma, J., Wang, H.: Cloud service description model: an extension of USDL for cloud services. IEEE Trans. Serv. Comput. 11, 354–368 (2015)
14. Galan, F., Sampaio, A., Rodero-Merino, L.: Service specification in cloud environments based on extensions to open standards. In: 4th International ICST Conference on COMmunication System softWAre and middlewaRE (COMSWARE 2009), no. 19, pp. 1–12. ACM, New York (2009)
15. Le, D., Nguyen, V., Goh, A.: Matching WSDL and OWL-S web services. In: IEEE International Conference on Semantic Computing, Berkeley, CA, pp. 197–202 (2009)
16. D'Ambrogio, A.: A model-driven WSDL extension for describing the QoS of Web services. In: IEEE International Conference on Web Services, pp. 789–796 (2006)
17. Chabeb, Y., Tata, S.: Yet another semantic annotation for WSDL. In: IADIS International Conference, Freiburg, Germany, pp. 437–441 (2008)
18. Sagayaraj, S., Santhoshkumar, M.: Transformation of complex type WSDL into OWL-S for facilitating SWS discovery. Int. J. Inf. Technol. 11(1), 5–12 (2018). https://doi.org/10.1007/s41870-018-0249-2

19. Martin, D., et al.: Bringing semantics to web services: the OWL-S approach. In: Cardoso, J., Sheth, A. (eds.) SWSWPC 2004. LNCS, vol. 3387, pp. 26–42. Springer, Heidelberg (2005). https://doi.org/10.1007/978-3-540-30581-1_4

20. Roman, D., et al.: WWW: WSMO, WSML, and WSMX in a nutshell. In: Mizoguchi, R., Shi, Z., Giunchiglia, F. (eds.) ASWC 2006. LNCS, vol. 4185, pp. 516–522. Springer, Heidelberg (2006). https://doi.org/10.1007/11836025_49

21. Gudenkauf, S., Josefiok, M., Göring, A.: A reference architecture for Cloud service offers. In: 2013 17th IEEE International Enterprise Distributed Object Computing Conference (EDOC), 9–13 September 2013, pp. 227–236. IEEE, Vancouver (2013)

22. Hoefer, C.N., Karagiannis, G.: Taxonomy of cloud computing services. In: 2010 IEEE Globecom Workshops, 6–10 December 2010, pp. 1345–1350. IEEE (2010)

23. Hoberg, P., Wollersheim, J., Krcmar, H.: Service descriptions for cloud services-the customers perspective. In: ConLife Academic Conference (2012)

24. Charfi, A., Schmeling, B., Novelli, F.: An overview of the unified service description language. In: 2010 IEEE 8th European Conference on Web Services (ECOWS), 1–3 December 2010, pp. 173–180. IEEE, Ayia Napa (2010)

25. Shetty, J., D'Mello, D.A.: An XML based data representation model to discover infrastructure services. In: 2015 International Conference on Smart Technologies and Management for Computing, Communication, Controls, Energy and Materials (ICSTM), 6–8 May 2015, pp. 119–125. IEEE, Chennai (2015)

26. Nagireddi, V.S.K., Mishra, S.: An ontology based cloud service generic search engine. In: 2013 8th International Conference on Computer Science & Education (ICCSE), 26–28 April 2013, pp. 335–340. IEEE, Colombo (2013)

27. Tahamtan, A., Beheshti, S.A., Anjomshoaa, A.: A cloud repository and discovery framework based on a unified business and Cloud service ontology. In: 2012 IEEE 8th World Congress on Services, 24–29 June 2012, pp. 203–210. IEEE, Honolulu (2012)

28. Alfazi, A., Sheng, Q.Z., Qin, Y.: Ontology-based automatic cloud service categorization for enhancing cloud service discovery. In: 2015 IEEE 19th International on Enterprise Distributed Object Computing Conference (EDOC), 21–25 September 2015, pp. 151–158. IEEE, Adelaide (2015)

29. Nguyen, D.K., Lelli, F., Papazoglou, M.P.: Blueprinting approach in support of cloud computing. Future Internet 4(1), 322–346 (2012)

30. Nguyen, D.K., Lelli, F., Taher, Y., Parkin, M., Papazoglou, M.P., van den Heuvel, W.-J.: Blueprint template support for engineering cloud-based services. In: Abramowicz, W., Llorente, I.M., Surridge, M., Zisman, A., Vayssière, J. (eds.) ServiceWave 2011. LNCS, vol. 6994, pp. 26–37. Springer, Heidelberg (2011). https://doi.org/10.1007/978-3-642-24755-2_3

31. OMG, MDA-The architecture of choice for a changing world. https://www.omg.org/mda/. Accessed 28 Mar 2021

32. Ghazouani, S., Slimani, Y.: A survey on cloud service description. J. Netw. Comput. Appl. 91, 61–74 (2017)

33. Nawaz, F., Mohsin, A., JanJua, N.K.: Service description languages in cloud computing: state-of-the-art and research issues. Serv. Oriented Comput. Appl. 13, 109–125 (2019)

34. Eclipse, Eclipse Modeling Framework (EMF). https://www.eclipse.org/modeling/emf/. Accessed 15 Jan 2021

A Novel Fault-Tolerant Approach to Web Service Composition upon the Edge Computing Environment

Tingyan Long[1], Peng Chen[2]($\boxtimes$), Yunni Xia[1]($\boxtimes$), Ning Jiang[3], Xu Wang[4], and Mei Long[5]

[1] Software Theory and Technology Chongqing Key Lab, Chongqing University, Chongqing 400044, China
xiayunni@hotmail.com
[2] School of Computer and Software Engineering, Xihua University, Chengdu, China
chenpeng@gkgb.com
[3] Mashang Consumer Finance Co., Ltd. (MSCF), Chongqing, China
[4] College of Mechanical Engineering, ChongQing University, Chongqing, China
[5] ZBJ NETWORK Co. Ltd., Chongqing, China

Abstract. In the edge environment, combining existing simple services to build value-added services that to meet users' needs has become a research hotspot of great practical value. With the increasing popularity of the edge computing paradigm, a large number of web services with similar functions have been created and deployed. Aiming at efficient and trustworthy composition of edge services, we proposed a novel fault-tolerant approach (FTSC) for edge service composition. Employs Primary-Backup (PB) fault-tolerant model to ensure edge service execution under the fault background, and leverages Deep-Q-learning-Network (DQN)-based algorithm for identifying the optimal service composition. For the validation purpose, we conducted extensive simulations based on the real dataset, which showed the proposed method clearly outperforms the traditional ones in terms of edge service completion rate, service active time and resource utilization.

Keywords: Edge computing · Fault tolerance · Service composition · Primary-backup · DQN

1 Introduction

As an emerging paradigm, the mobile edge computing MEC has extended cloud computing functions to the network edge [1], which can provide various application services to edge users. With the gradual maturity of edge computing technology, users' service needs are increasingly diversified and complicated. Service-Oriented Architecture (SOA) can integrate independent functional entities (i.e. services) that complete specific tasks in the network, which constructs a more complex value-added application (service composition) to meet the various needs

© Springer Nature Switzerland AG 2022
C. Xu et al. (Eds.): ICWS 2021, LNCS 12994, pp. 15–31, 2022.
https://doi.org/10.1007/978-3-030-96140-4_2

of users [2]. However, bandwidth limitations, resource constraints, and unpredictable edge computing environments may cause edge services to be unavailable. For example, during network switching, edge users are prone to network link disconnection and data packet loss. Excessive edge service requests result in slow service response speed and edge resource failure. Hence, in the edge computing environment, to ensure the reliable execution of composite services is an urgent problem to be solved. Redundancy technology is a key way to achieve service fault tolerance, which also makes composite services obtain high reliability and security. In [3], the authors studied time redundacy and space redundacy two fault tolerance mechanisms, with active replication strategy and passive replication strategy. In active strategy, it invokes all services and the first returned suitable one is used, whereas in passive strategy, the primary service is invoked first, then if it fails, a backup replication is used instead. The most popular reactive fault-tolerant method is the Primary-Backup (PB) method. Each abstract edge service in the PB model has a primary copy and a backup, all of which are placed on two separate edge nodes. If the primary service of the abstract service fails, the replica service is executed for compensation. Replication method has attracted more and more researchers' attention since fault-tolerant technology has become an effective method to ensure the reliable execution of composite services [4–8]. Although existing methods effectively guarantee the reliability of composite services, the problems of high time complexity and low efficiency still need to be solved.

Recently, with the increasing popularity and power of machine learning algorithms, reinforcement learning (RL) and Q-learning-based algorithms have received a lot of research. Many researchers have applied deep reinforcement learning methods to service composition [9–11]. However, the fault tolerance of service composition has not been involved in these research works. To tackle the above-mentioned problems, we propose a novel fault-tolerant service composition approach method by using a Deep Q-learning Network (DQN) and Primary-Backup (PB) fault-tolerant model, which is called FTSC. For the validation purpose, we conducted extensive simulations experiments which compared our method with other service composition fault-tolerant algorithms. The results show that FTSC method is superior to other algorithms in terms of service completion rate, service active time, and resource utilization.

2 Related Work

Fault-tolerant technology has become the most effective method to ensure the reliable execution of composite services, and has attracted more and more attention from researchers. For example, [5] proposed a redundancy-based fault-tolerant strategy to build a reliable service-oriented architecture SOA, proposed and implemented a fault-tolerant Web service-oriented distributed replication strategy evaluation and chose a frame. [4] defined users' requirements as local constraints and global constraints when constructing a reliable service-oriented system, and model the selection of fault-tolerant strategies as an optimization problem. Thus, a heuristic algorithm is proposed to effectively solve the optimization problem. [6] provided a compensation mechanism for the service composition language BPEL to roll back errors and proposed a method of automatically calculating the restoration plan based on genetic algorithms to ensure the satisfaction of the functional attributes after the restoration of the composite service. [9] employed the DDQN algorithm with prioritized replay to find optimal service composition solutions. [10] applied the long short-term memory (LSTM) neural networks in DQN to deal with the partially observable markov decision process (POMDP) problem in service composition, and the algorithm has adaptility for large-scale dynamic service composition.

With the development of edge computing, its architecture tends to be distributed and develops on a large scale. Therefore, when MEC is running massive computing-intensive tasks, it is prone to failures such as resource failure. DRL has already been used in web service composition, and a couple of work also dealt with web service composition based on DRL, but to the best of our knowledge, DRL has rarely been applied to fault-tolerant work in edge computing, with the exception of reference [8]. The fault-tolerant qos aware scheduling model in the edge cloud expands the traditional active and standby fault-tolerant model, and improves the service reliability of the edge cloud while meeting task time constraints.

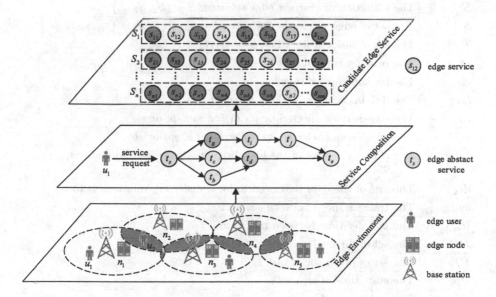

Fig. 1. A schematic diagram of edge environment

3   System Model and Constraint Analysis

3.1   Service Compostion Model

The edge computing environment generally refers to a collection of multiple edge servers deployed near the base station. Edge users' mobile devices are allowed to request service to near edge servers by wireless access point at any time and anywhere. Most of these services are short transactions (shorter execution time). e.g., news services, short video, audio services, transcoding services, and so on. As shown in Fig. 1. We use a set of $EN = \{n_1, n_2, ...\}$ to denote the collection of edge nodes deployed in corresponding edge nodes and $U = \{u_1, u_2, ...\}$ to denote the edge users. The edge environment provides a set of candidate edge services (abstract edge services) $S = \{S_1, S_2, ..., S_n\}$, each of which contains multiple concrete services, e.g., $S_1 = \{s_{11}, s_{12}, ..., s_{1m}\}$. Here, we assume that services

Table 1. Notations and description

Notation	Description
EN	The set of edge nodes, $EN = \{n_1, n_2, ...\}$
U	The collection of edge users, $U = \{u_1, u_2, ...\}$
S	The collection of abstract edge services, $S = \{S_1, S_2, ...\}$
S_i	The set of edge service in abstract edge service i, $S_i = \{s_{i1}, s_{i2}, ...\}$
T	The set of tasks in workflow, $T = \{t_1, t_2, ...\}$
pt_i	The primary copy of task t_i
bt_i	The backup copy of task t_i
$lx_i y_j$	The link between xt_i and yt_j where $x, y \in \{p, b\}$
sx_i	The edge service selected by pt_i or bt_i. i.e. sp_i or sb_i
sy_j	The edge service selected by pt_j or bt_j. i.e. sp_j or sb_j
$s_{hl}(xt_i)$	The lth edge service of the hth abstract edge service to tasks xt_i. $h \in S, l \in m$
$dv_{i,j}$	The size of the data that need to be transferred from task t_i to t_j
bw_{sx_i, sy_j}	The transfer speed between sx_i and sy_j
tt_{x_i, y_j}	The transfer time between task t_i and t_j
DP_i	The set of directed precursor of task t_i
PT_j	The set of precursor of task t_j
stp_i	The start time of pt_i
stb_i	The start time of bt_i
ftp_g	The finish time of pt_g
ftb_g	The finish time of bt_g
DT_j	The set of tasks in DP_j that cause t_j become weak primary copy
T_j	The set of tasks that comprises DT_j and tasks in PT_j which has caused t_i to become a weak primary copy

composition are expressed in terms of Directed acyclic graphs (DAG), which are composed of tasks that satisfy user's constraints. A DAG is represented by two tuples $W = (T, D)$, where $T = \{t_1, t_2, ..., t_n\}$ represents a set of tasks. $D = \{d_{i,j} | i, j \in [1, n]\}$ represents a set of precedence dependencies, where $d_{i,j} = 1$ means task t_j can be executed only when task t_i is completed, otherwise $d_{i,j} = 0$. In this paper, we use task to represent abstract edge service and edge user requests that service composition contains a plurality of edge services from candidate edge services (Table 1).

3.2 Constraint Analysis

According to the PB model, each task t_i has a primary copy pt_i and backup one bt_i, in which two different edge services are selected for fault tolerance. We assume the service size is measured by Million of Instructions (MI) [12]. We use $lx_i y_j$ to denote the link between xt_i and yt_j where $x, y \in \{p, b\}$, i.e., xt_i can be either pt_i or bt_i, and yt_j can be either pt_j or bt_j. For each link $lx_i y_j$, there is an associated data transfer time $tt_{x_i y_j}$ that is amount of time needed by yt_j from $s_{hl}(xt_i)$, where $h \in S$ and $l \in m$. Considering the proximity constraint of the edge environment and PB model, the transfer time between task t_i and t_j is:

$$tt_{x_i y_j} = \begin{cases} 0, & if \ sx_i = sy_j \\ \frac{dv_{i,j}}{bw_{sx_i, sy_j}}, & if \ sx_i \neq sy_j \end{cases} \tag{1}$$

where $sx_i = sy_j$ indicates that the edge service selected by the primary or replica of task t_i and the edge service selected by the primary or replica of task t_j belong to the same abstract service. $dv_{i,j}$ represents the size of the data that needs to be transferred from task t_i to t_j. bw_{sx_i, sy_j} denote the transfer speed between sx_i and sy_j.

To realize fault tolerance of service composition, we need to carry out constraint analysis on the selection of replica services. According to user u_1 request service composition, the set of directed precursor $DP_j = \{t_i\}$ and $DP_i = \{t_g\}$. The basic constraint refers to [13] for dependent tasks in DAG. A strong primary copy means that it can always receive results from its direct predecessors even if one of its direct predecessors fails. A weak primary copy is allowed to start before receiving the output data from the backups of its direct predecessors [18]. Figure 2 and Fig. 3 illustrated a strong primary case and weak primary case

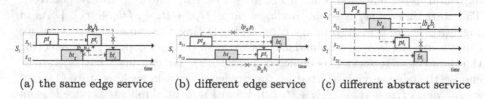

(a) the same edge service   (b) different edge service   (c) different abstract service

Fig. 2. Examples of t_i is strong primary service in three different cases, and the dashed lines with arrows represent message sent from parents to children.

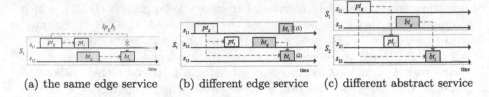

(a) the same edge service   (b) different edge service   (c) different abstract service

Fig. 3. Examples of t_i is weak primary service in three different cases, and the dashed lines with arrows represent message sent from parents to children.

respectively. It includes three situations, which are divided into selecting the same edge service as the previous task for the service copy, selecting different edge services in the same abstract service set, selecting edge services in different abstract services. We can know that the start time (stp_i) of pt_i is more than the finish time (ftb_g) of bt_g. However, due to the weak primary is defined as the finish time (ftb_g) of bt_g is more than the finish time (ftp_i) of pt_i. From Fig. 3(b), it is found that the replica service bt_i cannot select the edge service where the predecessor task pt_g is located, such as state (1), because t_i will fail when s_{11} fails.

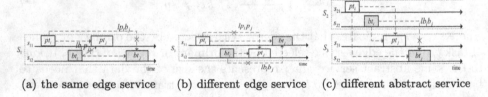

(a) the same edge service   (b) different edge service   (c) different abstract service

Fig. 4. pt_j is a strong primary copy and pt_i is a strong primary copy in three different cases

When pt_i is a strong primary copy, pt_j can be either a strong primary copy or a weak one, and it also contains three situations: the same edge service, different edge service, and different abstract service. Both pt_i and pt_j are strong primary, as shown in Fig. 4, and there are redundant connections in the three different scenarios, such as $lb_i p_j$, $lb_i b_j$. There are redundant connections $lp_i b_j$, $lb_i p_j$ and $lp_i p_j$, $lb_i b_j$ and $lb_i b_j$ in Fig. 4(a), Fig. 4(b), and Fig. 4(c) respectively. The start time of bt_j is equal to $stb_j = max\{ftp_i + tt_{p_i b_j}, ftb_i + tt_{b_i b_j}\}$. As in Fig. 5(a), pt_j is a weak primary copy and selecting the same edge service, we can observe the $lp_i b_j$ is a redundant link. A weak primary copy pt_j and selecting the different edge service as depicted in Fig. 5(b). We can find that bt_j cannot choose the edge service selected by the predecessor task, such as state (1), and $stb_j = max\{ftp_i + tt_{p_i b_j}, ftb_i + tt_{b_i b_j}\}$. From Fig. 5(c), duplicate service bt_j can only be found in the original abstract service collection $S3$, and the primary service cannot be selected.

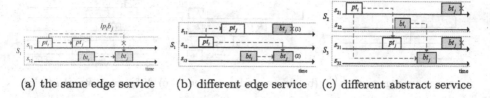

(a) the same edge service   (b) different edge service   (c) different abstract service

Fig. 5. pt_j is a weak primary copy and pt_i is a strong primary copy in three different cases

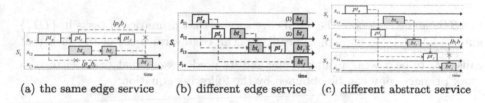

(a) the same edge service   (b) different edge service   (c) different abstract service

Fig. 6. t_j is strong primary copy and t_i is weak primary copy service in three different cases

When pt_i is a weak primary copy, pt_j can be either a strong primary copy or a weak primary one, and it also contains three situations. One is the same edge service, one is the different edge service, one is the different abstract service. Figure 6(a) indicates that pt_i is a weak primary copy and pt_j is a strong primary one, i.e., the same edge service. $lp_g b_i$ and $lp_i b_j$ are redundant links according to Fig. 3(a) and Fig. 4(a). Figure 6(b) describes that pt_i is a weak primary copy and pt_j is a strong one, i.e., the different edge service. bt_j can choose the edge service selected by the predecessor task, such as state (1) and state (2) on conditions that $stb_j > max\{ftp_i + tt_{p_i b_j}, ftb_i + tt_{b_i b_j}\}$. As shown in Fig. 6(c) illustrates that pt_i is a weak primary copy and pt_j is a strong primary one, i.e., the different abstract service. $lb_i b_j$ is a redundant link from Fig. 4(c). Figure 7(a) depicts that pt_i is a weak primary copy and pt_j is a weak primary one, i.e., the same edge service, we can know that $lp_i b_j$ is a redundant link. Different Fig. 6(b), the weak primary bt_j cannot choose the edge service selected by the predecessor task from Fig. 7(b).

After thinking over selecting edge service for service composition under the PB model, we will determine the set of available edge services where bt_j can be chosen considering all of its predecessors. Let DT_j denote the set of tasks in DP_j that cause t_j become weak primary copy. Suppose t_i be a task in DT_j, thus $DT_j = \{t_i\}$, T_j denote the set of tasks that comprises DT_j and tasks in PT_j which has caused t_i to become a weak primary copy. T_j can be determined by the following equation:

$$T_j = \{DT_j\} \cup \{\bigcup_{t_i \in DT_j} T_i\} \tag{2}$$

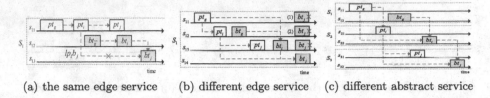

(a) the same edge service   (b) different edge service   (c) different abstract service

Fig. 7. t_j is weak primary copy and t_i is weak primary copy service in three different cases

Let SD_j and ST_i denote the set of edge service that primaries of tasks in $\{DT_j\}$ and $\{\underset{t_i \in DT_j}{\cup} T_i\}$ are chosen, respectively. The edge service set of the task that causes t_j to be a weak primary copy and its predecessors that cause t_j to be a weak primary copy can be obtained by the following equation:

$$SPT_j = \{SD_j\} \cup \{ST_i\} \cup \{sp_j\} \tag{3}$$

This equation indicates that bt_j cannot choose the edge services in SPT_j when pt_j is a weak primary copy, and the start time of bt_j must be no earlier than $\underset{t_i \in DT_j}{\max} \{ftb_i + tt_{b_i b_j}\}$.

3.3 Overlapping Mechanism

The overlapping mechanism refers to that one copy of an abstract service (task) overlaps with another. Figure 8 shows two cases of overlapping. In Fig. 8(a), when pt_i select edge service s_{12}, bt_g is cancelled that PB overlap from Fig. 3(b). In Fig. 8(b), when bt_i choose edge service s_{12}, pt_j is callcelled that PB overlap from Fig. 4(b) and bt_j cannot choose the edge service s_{11}. The case of multiple overlapped abstract service is shown in Fig. 9. As in Fig. 9(a), t_i is a weak primary copy and t_j is a strong primary copy. In this case, the task choose edge service is constrained by PB overlapping, i.e., if pt_j overlaps with a backup copy of it's predecessor, bt_j cannot choose the edge service in SPT_j according to Eq. (3). In Fig. 9(b), t_g, t_i and t_j are overlapped tasks. bt_j can not select edge service in SPT_j.

3.4 Problem Formulation

Based on the system model and fault-tolerant scenarios described above, we are interested in know how efficient, in terms of makespan and task completion rate of composite services in case of edge service failures, can the fault-tolerance strategy be. The resulting optimization problem is thus:

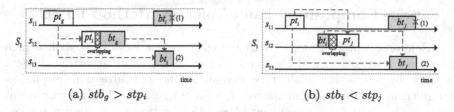

(a) $stb_g > stp_i$ (b) $stb_i < stp_j$

Fig. 8. An example of PB overlapping

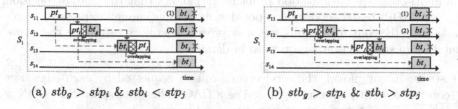

(a) $stb_g > stp_i$ & $stb_i < stp_j$ (b) $stb_g > stp_i$ & $stb_i > stp_j$

Fig. 9. An example of PB overlapping of multiple tasks

$$Minf = \sum_{k=1}^{U} FT_k \tag{4}$$

$$FT_k = \max_{t_j \in T}\{\lambda_{j,h,l} \cdot end_{yt_j} + \lambda_{j,h,l} \cdot end_{yt_j}\} \tag{5}$$

$$end_{yt_j} = \begin{cases} O_1(s_{hl}, yt_j), & PT(t_j) = \emptyset \\ \max\limits_{t_i \in PT(t_j)} \{end_{xt_i} + O_1(s_{hl}, yt_j)\}, & PT(t_j) \neq \emptyset \end{cases} \tag{6}$$

$$O_1(s_{hl}, yt_j) = \max_{t_i \in PT(t_j)} \{tt_{x_i y_j}\} \tag{7}$$

subject to:

$$k \in [1, U], \ h \in S, \ l \in m, x, y \in \{p, b\} \tag{8}$$

$$\lambda_{j,h,l} = \begin{cases} 1, & if \ yt_j \ choose \ edge \ service \ s_{hl} \\ 0, & oterwise \end{cases} \tag{9}$$

where f is the optimization objective, i.e., the makespan for multiple service composition, and FT_k refers to the finish time of the service composition from user u_k and $tt_{x_i y_j}$ is obtained from Eq. (1).

To solve this problem, we leverage a DQN-based framework for generating high-quality service fault-tolerant composition schemes. We regard the optimization objective as a DQN agent, the environment as a set of states and actions as given in the following sections.

4 Service Composition Fault-Tolerant Method FTSC

Deep Reinforcement Learning (DRL) is highly potent in dealing with a high dimensional state-space, and the main idea of DRL is that an artificial agent can learn by interacting with its environment and optimize multiple objectives given in the form of cumulative rewards [14,15]. The DQN environment includes components of environment observation, action space, policy setting, and reward design [16]. In addition, selecting edge services for abstract services is a multi-objective optimization problem. [11] shows that the Markov decision process (MDP)-based serviced composition model has enough expressive power to describe the control flow of a business process. Here, we introduce the representation of state, action, and reward in detail.

1) **state:** In our model, the service composition requested by each edge user consists of multiple tasks organized as a DAG. The state space $\mathcal{S}$ of DQN is the number of tasks with primary copy and backup one.
2) **action:** We define $\mathcal{A} = \{a_1, a_2, ..., a_n\}$ as the action space set and the number of optional actions is equal to the number of edge service in S.

Algorithm 1. Deep Q Learning algorithm

Input: W: the number of task, M: loop iteration, T: loop iteration
Output: scL, ESP, ESB
1: Initialize replay memory D to capacity N
2: Initialize action-value function Q with random weights
3: **for** $w = 1, W$ **do**
4:     $scL \leftarrow$ each task t_i be divided into primary copy pt_i and backup copy bt_i
5: **end for**
6: **for** $episode = 1, M$ **do**
7:     Initialise sequence $s_1 = \{t_1\}$ and preprocessed sequenced $\phi = \phi(s_i)$
8:     **for** $t = 1, T$ **do**
9:         With probability $epsilon$ select a random action a_t
10:         otherwise select $a_t = \max_a Q^*(\phi(s_t), a; \theta)$
11:         Execute action a_t in emulator observe reward r_t and state s_t
12:         Store transition $(\phi_t, a_t, r_t, \phi_{t+1})$ in D
13:         Sample random minibatch of transitions $(\phi_t, a_t, r_t, \phi_{t+1})$ from D
14:         Set $y_j = \begin{cases} r_j, & terminal\phi_{j+1} \\ r_j + \gamma \max_{a'} Q(\phi_{j+1}, a'; \theta), & non-terminal\phi_{j+1} \end{cases}$
15:         Perform a gradient descent step on $(y_j - Q(\phi_j, a_j; \theta)^2)$
16:     **end for**
17: **end for**
18: the best reward value as the final strategy, and select action of this strategy as the edge service selected by the task
19: $ESP \leftarrow$ the list of edge services selected by the primary copy of task
20: $ESB \leftarrow$ the list of edge services selected by the backup copy of task

---

3) reward: When agent i selects an edge service s_{hl}, agent i receive a reward which is an aggregate value for the QoS attributes of s_{hl}. This reward function $\mathcal{R}$ is expressed as:

$$r = \sum_{j=1}^{m} w \times \frac{Q_j - Q_j^{min}}{Q_j^{max} - q_j^{min}} + \varphi \tag{10}$$

where Q_j represents the observed value of the jth quality attribute of edge service s_{hl}, Q_j^{max} and Q_j^{min} represent the maximum and the minimum values of the jth quality attribute of edge service s_{hl}, respectively. w is a weighting factor. A boolean indicator φ indicates whether the edge service selected by the tasks' backup is in set SPT_j according to Eq. (3).

Next, we use the DQN [17] algorithm to find the optimal composition, where the optimization objective of Eq. (4) is the agent, and a reward R_t obtained by state s_t at time t as the input of the agent. After the agent learns from the environment, it generates a policy π_t. Based on the previous data and reward information, the policy π is a set that maps from state s_t to action u_t, which can be characterized as $\pi = f_t(a_t|s_t(n))$. Afterwards, the agent takes any action of a_t according to π_t, and the environment feeds back the next state s_{t+1} and the corresponding reward r_{t+1} to the agent as the response. Here, the reward function can be obtained as the maximum value under the optimal policy $\pi_t(s)$:

$$\pi_t(s) = \arg\max_a Q^\pi(s, a) \tag{11}$$

where $\pi_t'(s)$ is obtained from the expectation of the accumulated future reward. The value function is updated according to the time difference:

$$Q(s, a) = (1 - \alpha)Q(s, a) + \alpha[R(a) + \gamma \max_{a' \in A} Q(s', a')] \tag{12}$$

in which $Q(s, a)$ is the state-action value function at the current state, $Q(s', a')$ is the state-action value function at the next state, α is the update step size, $R(a)$ is the reward according to Eq. (10), and γ is the reward decay factor. The loss function of DQN is

$$\mathcal{L}(\theta) = E_{s,a,r,s'}[y - (Q(s, a|\theta))^2] \tag{13}$$

$$y = R(a) + \delta \max_{a' \in A} Q(s', a') \tag{14}$$

in which y denotes the target Q-value that the current Q-value is approaching. The pseudocode of the DQN with experience playback and target network is illustrated in Algorithm 1. The target network prevents the instabilities to propagate quickly and reduces the risk of divergence. The replay memory keeps all information for the last $N_{replay} \in \mathcal{N}$ time steps, where the experience is collected by applying an ϵ-greedy policy. The updates are then made on a set of tuples

$<s, a, r, s'>$ selected randomly within the replay memory. It allows for updates that cover a wide range of the state-action space and provides the possibility to make a larger update of the parameters while having an efficient parallelization of the algorithm.

Algorithm 2. Fault Tolerant Service Composition Algorithm in FTSC

1: Schedule tasks according to the scheduling strategy obtained in Alogrithm 1
2: scL, ESP, ESB from Alogrithm 1
3: **while** $scL \neq Null$ **do**
4:      $ft=+\infty$;
5:      select the first abstract service (task) t_i from scL;
6:      **if** edge service s_{hl} in $ESP \neq$ failed **then**
7:          calculate the earliest start time stp_i;
8:          $ftp_i \leftarrow stp_i + e(pt_i)$;
9:          **if** $ftp_i \leq ft_i - e(pt_i)$ **then**
10:              **if** $ftp_i < ft$ **then**
11:                  $ft \leftarrow ftp_i$;
12:              **end if**
13:          **end if**
14:      **else**
15:          **if** edge service s_{hl} in $ESB \neq$ failed **then**
16:              calculate the start time stb_i;
17:              $ftb_i \leftarrow stb_i + e(bt_i)$;
18:              **if** $ftb_i \leq ft_i - e(bt_i)$ **then**
19:                  **if** $ftb_i < ft$ **then**
20:                      $ft \leftarrow ftb_i$;
21:                  **end if**
22:              **end if**
23:          **end if**
24:      **end if**
25: **end while**

As illustrated in Algorithm 2, the overall composition algorithm, i.e., FTSC, invokes the DQN-based one given in Algorithm 1. It aims to select the optimal edge service for the service composition requested by the user and to make the service composition fault tolerant. Due to each task in the DAG is split into two copies, i.e., a primary copy and a backup one, the algorithm divides the deadline into sub-deadline for all tasks according to [18]. Consequently, each task $t_i(1 \leq i \leq n)$ in DAG has an individual time window with start time st_i, sub-deadline dt_i, and finish time ft_i of task t_i. stb_i, ftb_i and $\tilde{d}t_i$ denote the start time, finish time, and sub-deadline time of t_i's backup copy. Tasks is considered as faulty if $ft_i > dt_i$ or $ftb_i > \tilde{d}t_i$. $e(pt_i)$ and $e(bt_i)$ means the response time of task pt_i and $e(bt_i)$. Then, according to Algorithm 1 obtain scheduling strategy, finishing edge services primary copies as early as possible and evenly distributing primary copies among edge service to shorten service response time.

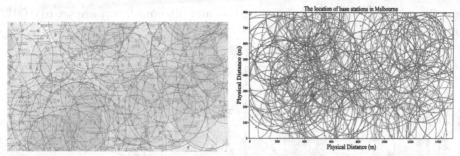

(a) The edge service deployment on the Google Map (b) The edge service deployment shown on the coordinates

Fig. 10. An example of edge services with their deployment

5   Experiments

5.1   Experiment Setting

In simulative experiments, we assume edge services and edge users are located according to the EUA dataset [19] as illustrated in Fig. 10. The service composite is expressed in the form of multiple service composition templates as given in Fig. 11. The experiment is based on two real service datasets QWS and WS-DREAM's QoSDataset2. The QWS [20] dataset contains 2507 real Web services, and each service contains 9 QoS attributes. WS-DREAM's QoS [21] dataset contains response time and throughput of 339 users using 5825 Web services. In the experiment, four QoS attributes are considered, which are availability, reliability, response time and throughput.

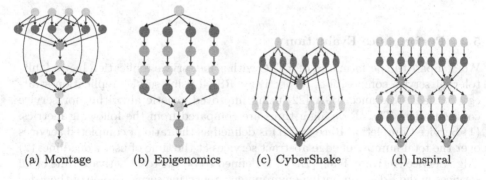

(a) Montage   (b) Epigenomics   (c) CyberShake   (d) Inspiral

Fig. 11. Service composition templates

We use TensorFlow to implement the DQN in simulation test and we use a workstation with the 2.9 GHz, Intel(R)Core(TM)i5.9400F, and 16.0 GB RAM configuration. The parameter settings of DQN are listed in Table 2. According to as illustrated in Fig. 12, the learning rate and discount factor are set to 0.001 and 0.6.

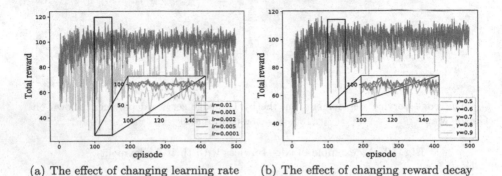

(a) The effect of changing learning rate   (b) The effect of changing reward decay

Fig. 12. The effect of varying learning rate and reward decay

Table 2. The parameters used in the experiment

Parameter	Value	Description
ϵ	0.3	The probability of selecting random action
min_ϵ	0.05	The minimum value of ϵ
$batch\_size$	200	Sample size in each step
$memory\_size$	10000	The sizes of samples
$\epsilon\_decrement$	0.00001	The decrease of ϵ each time
$replace\_target\_iter$	200	The update of network parameter at interval

5.2 Performance Evaluation

We compare the performance of FTSC with some service replication based fault-tolerant service composition, respectively. RS [4] using service replication strategy for fault tolerance. rGA [22] using improved genetic algorithm for service compensation. The above algorithms are compared from the following metrics: (1) Service Completion Rate (SCR) is defined as the ratio of completed services over the total number of edge abstract services at the time of user's deadline. (2) Edge Service Activate Time (EST) is defined to be the total activate time of all services in the Edge computing environment, reflecting service usage of the Edge computing environment. (3) Ratio of abstract edge service over Service activate time (RTS) is defined to be the ratio of the total tasks' response time over the total activate time of services, reflecting utilization of the edge environment. In this work, we focus on the failure of edge service, the faults are assumed to be independent, affecting only a single edge service. Figure 13 shows the comparison of service completion rate of different method with some well-known scientific computing flow templates [23]. As can be seen from Fig. 13, the service completion rate of FTSC is higher than that of its peers (e.g., Fig. 13(a), 6.62%, 11%, when $DAG = 150$), and then the EST is lower as well than those of its peers. Moreover, Fig. 13(c) shows the RTS of FTSC have higher utilization rate than its peers.

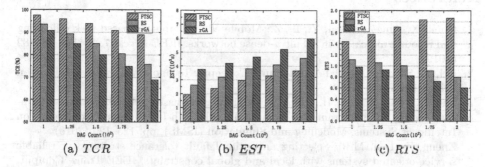

(a) TCR (b) EST (c) RTS

Fig. 13. Performance with varying numbers of service composition

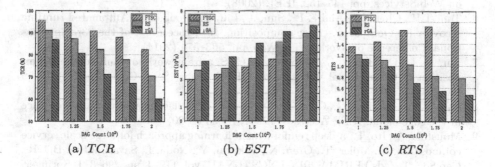

(a) TCR (b) EST (c) RTS

Fig. 14. Performance with varying numbers of randomly gernerated DAGs.

As shown in Fig. 14(a), our proposed method achieves higher service completion rate (8.35%, 19.56% when DAG = 150) than those of its peers for random workflow template, and the comparison shows a similar pattern to that of Fig. 13, i.e., FTSC exhibits higher performance in terms of edge service time and utilization.

6 Conclusion

In this paper, we propose a novel fault-tolerant method for service composition in the edge environment. The proposed method FTSC is capable of handling faults of edge service by employing an extended primary-backup model and a

Q-learning-based strategy for yielding optimal service composition solutions. To validate our proposed approach, we conducted a simulatiion case study based on a well-known edge-service-position dataset and QoS dataset and demonstrate that our method shows a better tolerance to the increase of user's requests, suggesting its good scalability.

References

1. Chen, X., Liu, Z., Chen, Y., Li, Z.: Mobile edge computing based task offloading and resource allocation in 5G ultra-dense networks. IEEE Access **7**, 184172–184182 (2019)
2. Erl, T.: Service-Oriented Architecture: Concepts, Technology, and Design. Pearson Education, India (1900)
3. Shu, Y., Wu, Z., Liu, H., Gao, Y.: A simulation-based reliability analysis approach of the fault-tolerant web services. In: 2016 7th International Conference on Intelligent Systems, Modelling and Simulation (ISMS), pp. 125–129 (2016)
4. Zheng, Z., Lyu, M.R.: Selecting an optimal fault tolerance strategy for reliable service-oriented systems with local and global constraints. IEEE Trans. Comput. **64**(1), 219–232 (2014)
5. Zheng, Z., Lyu, M.R.: A distributed replication strategy evaluation and selection framework for fault tolerant web services. In: 2008 IEEE International Conference on Web Services, pp. 145–152. IEEE (2008)
6. Tan, T.H., Chen, M., André, É., Sun, J., Liu, Y., Dong, J.S.: Automated runtime recovery for QoS-based service composition. In: Proceedings of the 23rd International Conference on World Wide Web, pp. 563–574 (2014)
7. Liu, A., Li, Q., Huang, L., Xiao, M.: FACTS: a framework for fault-tolerant composition of transactional web services. IEEE Trans. Serv. Comput. **3**(1), 46–59 (2009)
8. Sun, H., Yu, H., Fan, G., Chen, L.: QoS-aware task placement with fault-tolerance in the edge-cloud. IEEE Access **8**, 77987–78003 (2020)
9. Moustafa, A., Ito, T.: A deep reinforcement learning approach for large-scale service composition. In: Miller, T., Oren, N., Sakurai, Y., Noda, I., Savarimuthu, B.T.R., Cao Son, T. (eds.) PRIMA 2018. LNCS (LNAI), vol. 11224, pp. 296–311. Springer, Cham (2018). https://doi.org/10.1007/978-3-030-03098-8_18
10. Wang, H., et al.: Adaptive and large-scale service composition based on deep reinforcement learning. Knowl.-Based Syst. **180**, 75–90 (2019)
11. Doshi, P., Goodwin, R., Akkiraju, R., Verma, K.: Dynamic workflow composition: using Markov decision processes. Int. J. Web Serv. Res. (IJWSR) **2**(1), 1–17 (2005)
12. Calheiros, R.N., Ranjan, R., Beloglazov, A., De Rose, C.A., Buyya, R.: CloudSim: a toolkit for modeling and simulation of cloud computing environments and evaluation of resource provisioning algorithms. Softw.: Pract. Exp. **41**(1), 23–50 (2011)
13. Zhu, X., Wang, J., Guo, H., Zhu, D., Yang, L.T., Liu, L.: Fault-tolerant scheduling for real-time scientific workflows with elastic resource provisioning in virtualized clouds. IEEE Trans. Parallel Distrib. Syst. **27**(12), 3501–3517 (2016)
14. Cui, D., Ke, W., Peng, Z., Zuo, J.: Multiple DAGs workflow scheduling algorithm based on reinforcement learning in cloud computing. In: Li, K., Li, J., Liu, Y., Castiglione, A. (eds.) ISICA 2015. CCIS, vol. 575, pp. 305–311. Springer, Singapore (2016). https://doi.org/10.1007/978-981-10-0356-1_31

15. Jiahao, W., Zhiping, P., Delong, C., Qirui, L., Jieguang, H.: A multi-object optimization cloud workflow scheduling algorithm based on reinforcement learning. In: Huang, D.-S., Jo, K.-H., Zhang, X.-L. (eds.) ICIC 2018. LNCS, vol. 10955, pp. 550–559. Springer, Cham (2018). https://doi.org/10.1007/978-3-319-95933-7_64
16. Mnih, V., et al.: Playing Atari with deep reinforcement learning. arXiv preprint arXiv:1312.5602 (2013)
17. Mnih, V., et al.: Human-level control through deep reinforcement learning. Nature 518(7540), 529–533 (2015)
18. Qin, X., Jiang, H.: A novel fault-tolerant scheduling algorithm for precedence constrained tasks in real-time heterogeneous systems. Parallel Comput. 32(5/6), 331–356 (2006)
19. Lai, P., et al.: Optimal edge user allocation in edge computing with variable sized vector bin packing. In: Pahl, C., Vukovic, M., Yin, J., Yu, Q. (eds.) ICSOC 2018. LNCS, vol. 11236, pp. 230–245. Springer, Cham (2018). https://doi.org/10.1007/978-3-030-03596-9_15
20. Zheng, Z., Zhang, Y., Lyu, M.R.: Investigating QoS of real-world web services. IEEE Trans. Serv. Comput. 7(1), 32–39 (2012)
21. Al Masri, E., Mahmoud, Q.H.: Discovering the best web service. In: Proceedings of the 16th international conference on World Wide Web, pp. 1257–1258 (2007)
22. Tian, H.T., Chen, M., Étienne André, Sun, J., Jin, S.D.: Automated runtime recovery for QoS-based service composition. In: International Conference on World Wide Web (2014)
23. Deelman, E., et al.: Pegasus, a workflow management system for science automation. Futur. Gener. Comput. Syst. 46, 17–35 (2015)

A Novel High-Order Cluster-GCN-Based Approach for Service Recommendation

Man Luo[1], Peng Chen[2], Tianhao Sun[1], Yunni Xia[1(✉)], Ning Jiang[3],
Xu Wang[4], and Wei Wei[5]

[1] School of computers, Chongqing University, Chongqing 400030, China
xiayunni@hotmail.com
[2] School of Computer and Software Engineering, Xihua University,
Chengdu 610039, China
[3] Mashang Consumer Finance Co., Ltd. (MSCF), Chongqing 400021, China
[4] College of Mechanical Engineering, Chongqing University,
Chongqing 400030, China
[5] School of Computer Science and Engineering, Xi'an University of Technology,
Xi'an 710048, China

Abstract. When exploring high-order neighbors for embedding learning, data sparsity problems in service recommendation system can be compensated via Graph Convolutional Network (GCN). However, the performance of GCN will deteriorate when stacking more layers, namely, over-smoothing problem. Though LightGCN and LR-GCN can alleviate over-smoothing and achieve state-of-the-art performance, all users with dissimilar preferences become similar and the services become homogeneous, introducing noise information in exploration high-order graph convolution. Thus, we argue that the loss of uniqueness of all nodes is the cause of over-smoothing problems in high-order graph convolution. To solve the above problems, we propose to use graph clustering algorithm to cluster user-service graph. Moreover, this node enhancement technique in our model can further facilitate systems to learn more information from nearby neighbors. The experimental results confirm that the proposed algorithm outperforms most baseline algorithms, achieving state-of-the-art performance.

Keywords: Service recommendation · Graph convolution networks · Clustering

1 Introduction

Service recommendation refers to a proactive service-discovery technique, which actively pushes services to users according to users' preferences. By analyzing user's historical interactions with services such as service choosing and ratings, service recommendation system can predict what service the user might interact

---

M. Luo and P. Chen—Contribute equally to this work and thus are co-first authors.

© Springer Nature Switzerland AG 2022
C. Xu et al. (Eds.): ICWS 2021, LNCS 12994, pp. 32–45, 2022.
https://doi.org/10.1007/978-3-030-96140-4_3

with next. With the assumption that users with similar service choosing tendency will show a similar preference upon services, collaborate filtering (CF) [1] is proposed to perform recommendation tasks. Users and services are parameterized according to the historical records, and predictions are made based on these parameters. There are many previous works making effort to improve performance of recommendation. For example, matrix factorization (MF) [2] directly projected the ID of each user (or service) embedding, conducting inner product between them; neural recommendation models like NeuCF [3] improve performance by using neural networks instead of MF interaction function of inner product; ACF [4] and NAIS [5] utilize attention mechanisms, automatically capturing the different contributions between different services.

GCN is a neural network specializing in learning graph data with non-Euclidean structure, and widely used in recommendation tasks. GCN-based model, NGCF [6], was proposed to further exploit subgraph structure with high-hop neighbors and achieve state-of-art performance for CF. However, NGCF suffers from over-smoothing problem, because the multi-layer graph convolution operation makes node representation become indistinguishable. As a result, the peak performance of most current GCN-based models is obtained by stacking only 2 or 3 layers, and the further addition of layers will cause performance degradation. Removing nonlinear activation in the NGCF is adopted to simplify the network structure for solving this problem in some models such as LR-GCCF [7], this model introduces the residual network structure to alleviate the problem of over-smoothing and improve the recommendation performance. In addition to LR-GCCF, LightGCN [8] was also proposed and it improved performance by removing feature transformation and nonlinear activation. Although some GCN-based models are expected to alleviate over-smoothing problem, indiscriminately aggregating the information of all neighbor nodes will make dissimilar users more and more similar, making model learn some redundant information, which will eventually lead models to over-smoothing. Finding a new approach to fix this issue is in great need.

Here, we propose a novel service recommendation model named High-order Cluster GCN (HC-GCN), which uses a clustering algorithm to partition all users and services into several subgraphs, and then performs graph convolution operations on nodes inside the subgraphs. Unlike IMP-GCN [9], which generates subgraph by additional neural network, HC-GCN partitions graph with an efficient algorithm METIS [10], which aims to build partitions on the vertices (users and services) of the graph so that there are more intra-cluster links than inter-cluster links. Our model is based on the assumption that users in the same cluster (subgraph) have similar preferences, and the inter-cluster links are negative information in the propagation of graph convolution. Therefore, our model can also reduce the possibility of users becoming more and more similar during the embedding learning, and finally achieve the goal of alleviating the over-smoothing problem. Experimental results using our model show that significantly outperform LightGCN. Our results confirm that HC-GCN is an efficient approach to overcome over-smoothing problems, paving the way of practically using highly efficient service recommendation systems in the future.

2   Related Work

2.1   Collaborative Filtering

Collaborative filtering (CF) is a principal technique in recommendation systems. CF models parameterize users and services as embeddings by learning from historical embeddings. For example, MF [2,11] conducts inner product between user and service embeddings, which are ID embedding of each user and service. Then neural recommendation models like NeuCF [3] improve performance by adding neural networks to the embedding component. SVD++ [12] uses the weighted average value of historical services ID embedding as the embedding of target users. Recently, considering different services that should contribute differently to people's personalized preference, ACF [4] and NAIS [5] use attention mechanisms automatically capturing the distinctive contributions.

2.2   Graph Methods for Recommendation

Graph-based methods and embedding-based methods are combined to learn the representation of users and services. However, only used to enrich the training data, the HOP-Rec [13] has no direct effect on the model, therefore, higher-order connectivity has not been fully explored. Furthermore, using random walks takes additional computational costs to adjust parameters. To lead the embedding learning, Graph neural networks (GNNs) [14,15] are essential for the modeling of graph structure, particularly high-hop neighbors. Spectral CNN [16] applies Laplace spectrum to graph, and proposes the convolution kernel in the spectral domain. Vanilla GCN [15] further expands the spectral graph convolutions through several simplifications.

The advantages of graph convolution have attracted many researchers [6,17,18] to apply GCN to user-service bigraph to capture features in high-order neighbors for a recommendation. Later-proposed SGCN [19] folded multiple weight matrices into one and eliminating nonlinearities, simplifying complicated and redundant GCN. This model later inspires the development of LR-GCCF and LightGCN. They are only designing the model to solve the over-smoothing problem from the perspective of graph convolution, rather than the recommended domain. Thus, later-developed IMP-GCN proposes that the reason for the over-smoothing problem is to explore higher-order neighbor nodes indiscriminately, and they restricted embedding propagation to a subgraph with similar interests. Nevertheless, IMP-GCN introduces a three-layer graph generation network model in order to generate subgraphs, adding too much burden to the model. In this paper, we use a more efficient graph clustering algorithm to generate subgraphs, which filters out the negative information of embedding learning in the high-order graph convolution operation. Our model efficiently overcomes the over-smoothing problems.

3 Method

3.1 Recap

The interaction and affiliation data can be represented by an undirected graph $G = (\mathcal{V}, \mathcal{E}, A)$, where $\mathcal{V}$ consists of users $u \in U$ and services $i \in I$, A is the adjacency matrix. If it exits an interaction between u and i, each entry R_{ui} is 1, otherwise, it is 0. $R \in \mathbb{R}^{M \times N}$ is the interaction matrix between services and users. The adjacency matrix of the user-service bigraph is:

$$A = \begin{pmatrix} 0 & R \\ R^T & 0 \end{pmatrix}. \tag{1}$$

In this paper, because LightGCN with light design achieves state-of-the-art performance in the graph-based recommendation model, we will briefly introduce it. Our model bases on the design of LightGCN. Typically, $e_u^{(0)}$ ($e_i^{(0)}$) is the ID embedding of user u (service i). For LightGCN, the graph convolution operation is defined as:

$$e_u^{(k+1)} = \sum_{i \in \mathcal{N}_u} \frac{1}{\sqrt{|\mathcal{N}_u|}\sqrt{|\mathcal{N}_i|}} e_i^{(k)},$$
$$e_i^{(k+1)} = \sum_{u \in \mathcal{N}_i} \frac{1}{\sqrt{|\mathcal{N}_i|}\sqrt{|\mathcal{N}_u|}} e_u^{(k)}, \tag{2}$$

where $e_u^{(k)}$ ($e_i^{(k)}$) is the embedding of user u (service i) generated from previous k layers propagation. $\mathcal{N}_u$ and $\mathcal{N}_i$ are first-order neighbors that user u and the service i have interacted. $\frac{1}{\sqrt{|\mathcal{N}_u|}\sqrt{|\mathcal{N}_i|}}$ is symmetric normalization term designed by standard GCN [15], which is proposed to address the problem that graph convolution operation increases embedding scale.

$$e_u = \sum_{k=0}^{K} \alpha_k e_u^{(k)}; \quad e_i = \sum_{k=0}^{K} \alpha_k e_i^{(k)}, \tag{3}$$

where $\alpha_k \geq 0$, indicates the importance of the k-th layer embedding. α_k is uniformly defined as $1/(K+1)$. Model iteratively updates nodes by aggregating high-order neighbor feature information, and each node is becoming more and more homogeneous, losing individual characteristics, and finally causing over-smoothing problems. All models start to over-smoothing after aggregating high-order neighbors, which means that high-order neighbors with noisy information hinder learning a better embedding. For example, users' preferences in high-order neighbors are different or even contradictory, which are employed to update the target node embedding in graph convolution operations. IMP-GCN has proved through experiments that after 6-layer or 7-layer graph convolution, a node can aggregate information from all other nodes through message passing, so continuous aggregation of higher-order neighbors would inevitably cause over-smoothing problems. In recommendation, it means users lose personalization in the deep graph structure, and all services become homogeneous.

At present, GCN-based models in recommendation obtain the peak performance at 3rd or 4th layer. From the user's perspective, the reason for inferior performance is that some user groups are interested in a series of services, and different user groups may hold opposite attitudes to this series of services. Therefore, without distinguishing user groups, opposite preferences within the groups are possibly propagated together during the graph convolution operation, introducing negative information in iteratively updating the target node. To solve the above problems, it is necessary to partition the user subgraphs in the high-order graph convolution operation, which partitions users with similar preferences into one subgraph and constrains the embedding propagation in one subgraph. By partitioning the subgraph, the number of high-order neighbors and negative information is reduced, thereby alleviating the over-smoothing.

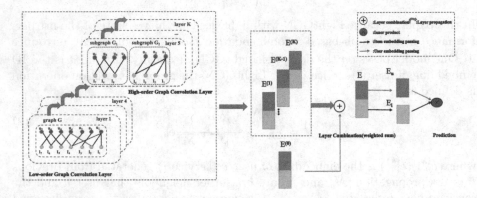

Fig. 1. An illustration of HC-GCN with two subgraphs as example. In HC-GCN, the first four-order propagation operations on graph G, and high-order propagation operations inside the subgraphs $\bar{G}$.

3.2   HC-GCN Model

In this section, we present our model HC-GCN in detail, and the structure of HC-GCN model is shown in Fig. 1, which mainly consists of three parts: 1) graph convolution; 2) layer combination; and 3) model prediction. Mentioning graph convolution, we illustrate how to cluster the users and services into different subgraph.

Clustering. HC-GCN uses subgraphs instead of the entire graph in the graph convolution operation to filter negative information. Therefore, we need to partition the subgraphs through the user-service bigraph. Unlike IMP-GCN, HC-GCN uses all nodes to guide the subgraphs partition. We deem that all nodes become homogeneous in iteratively updating the embedding through the high-order neighbor embedding. The subgraph partitioned from the perspective of user preference is not comprehensive enough, and the service node should only belong to one of the subgraphs. We use METIS to partition the graph into several subgraphs, realizing that each node belongs to only one of the subgraphs.

We partition user-service nodes into c groups: $\mathcal{V} = [\mathcal{V}_1, \cdots \mathcal{V}_c]$ where $\mathcal{V}_t$ consists of the users and services in the t-th partition. Then there are c user-service subgraphs as:

$$\bar{G} = [G_1, \cdots, G_c] = [\{\mathcal{V}_1, \mathcal{E}_1\}, \cdots, \{\mathcal{V}_c, \mathcal{E}_c\}], \tag{4}$$

where each $\mathcal{E}_t$ consists of the interactions between users and services in $\mathcal{V}_t$. After reorganizing users and services, the adjacency matrix is partitioned into c^2 submatrices as:

$$A = \bar{A} + \Delta = \begin{bmatrix} A_{11} & \cdots & A_{1c} \\ \vdots & \ddots & \vdots \\ A_{c1} & \cdots & A_{cc} \end{bmatrix} \tag{5}$$

and

$$\bar{A} = \begin{bmatrix} A_{11} & \cdots & 0 \\ \vdots & \ddots & \vdots \\ 0 & \cdots & A_{cc} \end{bmatrix}, \Delta = \begin{bmatrix} 0 & \cdots & A_{1c} \\ \vdots & \ddots & \vdots \\ A_{c1} & \cdots & 0 \end{bmatrix}, \tag{6}$$

each diagonal block A_{tt} contains links within G_t which is a $|\mathcal{V}_t| \times |\mathcal{V}_t|$ adjacency matrix. $\bar{A}$ denotes the adjacency matrix of graph $\bar{G}$; A_{st} includes the links between $\mathcal{V}_s$ and $\mathcal{V}_t$; Δ matrix is all non-diagonal block parts of A.

Graph Convolution (GC). Since LightGCN began to suffer from over-smoothing in the 4th or 5th layer, the interaction between the first 3 or 4 orders users and services should be positive for learning better embedding representations. Graph convolution is mainly composed of two parts: lower-order graph convolution and higher-order graph convolution.

Lower-order Graph Convolution. In the first four-order propagation layers, the graph convolution operation should involve whole graph G. Additionally, nearby neighbors should contribute more than distant nodes, thus, we proposed a technique named node enhancement and inspired by paper [20], which gives greater weight to nearby neighbors and is capable of capturing more information from neighboring nodes in learning embedding. $e_u^{(k)}$ ($e_i^{(k)}$) is the embedding of user u (service i) after k layers graph convolution operation. The first four-order graph convolution can be:

$$e_u^{(k+1)} = \sum_{i \in \mathcal{N}_u} \left(\frac{1}{\sqrt{|\mathcal{N}_u|}\sqrt{|\mathcal{N}_i|}} + \frac{1}{\sqrt{|\mathcal{N}_u|}} \right) e_i^{(k)},$$
$$e_i^{(k+1)} = \sum_{u \in \mathcal{N}_i} \left(\frac{1}{\sqrt{|\mathcal{N}_u|}\sqrt{|\mathcal{N}_i|}} + \frac{1}{\sqrt{|\mathcal{N}_i|}} \right) e_u^{(k)}, \tag{7}$$

where $\mathcal{N}_u$ and $\mathcal{N}_i$ are first-order neighbors of user u and the service i in whole graph G.

Higher-order Graph Convolution. For higher-order graph convolution layers, the iterative update of a node embedding is only related to its neighbors in its subgraph to filter negative and noisy information. The graph convolution of higher-order HC-GCN is:

$$e_u^{(k+1)} = \sum_{i \in \mathcal{N}_u'} \left(\frac{1}{\sqrt{|\mathcal{N}_u'|}\sqrt{|\mathcal{N}_i'|}} + \frac{1}{\sqrt{|\mathcal{N}_u'|}} \right) e_i^{(k)},$$

$$e_i^{(k+1)} = \sum_{u \in \mathcal{N}_i'} \left(\frac{1}{\sqrt{|\mathcal{N}_u'|}\sqrt{|\mathcal{N}_i'|}} + \frac{1}{\sqrt{|\mathcal{N}_i'|}} \right) e_u^{(k)},$$

(8)

where $\mathcal{N}_u'$ and $\mathcal{N}_i'$ are first-order neighbors of user u and the service i in subgraphs $\bar{G}$ (mentioned in (4)).

Layer Combination and Prediction. After K-layers graph convolution, the embeddings collected in each layer are combined to form the final representation of the user (the service), defined as (3).

We conduct inner product between users (e.g. e_u) and services (e.g. e_i) final embedding to predict the preference of user to the target service:

$$\hat{y}_{ui} = \mathbf{e}_u^T \mathbf{e}_i$$

(9)

Matrix Form. Set the 0-th layer embedding matrix to be $E^{(0)} \in \mathbb{R}^{(M+N) \times d_k}$, where M and N are the numbers of users and services, respectively, d_k denotes the embedding size.

The first four-order graph convolution matrix form of the model is:

$$E^{(k+1)} = \left(D^{-\frac{1}{2}} A D^{-\frac{1}{2}} + D^{-\frac{1}{2}} \right) E^{(k)}.$$

(10)

The higher-order graph convolution matrix form of the model is:

$$E^{(k+1)} = \left(\bar{D}^{-\frac{1}{2}} \bar{A} \bar{D}^{-\frac{1}{2}} + \bar{D}^{-\frac{1}{2}} \right) E^{(k)},$$

(11)

where D and $\bar{D}$ note a diagonal matrix $(M + N) \times (M + N)$ in the G and $\bar{G}$, respectively, the t-th diagonal element $D_{tt} = |\mathcal{N}_t|$ in the graph G, the t-th diagonal element $\bar{D}_{tt} = |\mathcal{N}_t'|$ in the graph $\bar{G}$, $\bar{A}$ (mentioned in (6)) denotes the adjacency matrix of subgraphs $\bar{G}$.

Final embedding matrix of HC-GCN is applied for model prediction as:

$$E = \alpha_0 E^{(0)} + \alpha_1 E^{(1)} + \alpha_2 E^{(2)} + \ldots + \alpha_K E^{(K)}$$
$$= \alpha_0 E^{(0)} + \alpha_1 \tilde{A} E^{(0)} + \ldots + \alpha_5 \tilde{A}'^5 E^{(0)} + \ldots + \alpha_K \tilde{A}'^K E^{(0)},$$

(12)

where $\tilde{A} = D^{-\frac{1}{2}} A D^{-\frac{1}{2}}$ and $\tilde{A}' = \bar{D}^{-\frac{1}{2}} \bar{A} \bar{D}^{-\frac{1}{2}}$ are the symmetrically normalized matrix in the whole graph G and subgraphs $\bar{G}$, respectively.

3.3 Model Training

Since pairwise Bayesian Personalized Ranking (BPR) loss [21] has been widely adopted in recommendation systems, it is chosen to learn model parameters. BPR assumes that negative services that better show user preferences should be assigned higher predictive values than negative services. The objective function is:

$$L_{BPR} = -\sum_{u=1}^{M} \sum_{i \in \mathcal{N}_u} \sum_{j \notin \mathcal{N}_u} \ln \sigma \left(\hat{y}_{ui} - \hat{y}_{uj} \right) + \lambda \left\| \mathrm{E}^{(0)} \right\|^2 \qquad (13)$$

The trainable parameters of our model are embeddings of the 0-th layer $E^{(0)}$, where λ controls the regularization intensity of $L2$. We use the mini-batch Adam [22] optimizer to update our model parameters.

4 Experimental Analysis

We conducted experiments on four real datasets to evaluate the effectiveness of our proposed method. Our goal is to answer the following research questions:

- RQ1: How does HC-GCN perform compared with state-of-the-art CF methods?
- RQ2: How do different variants designs (e.g., node enhancement technique, cluster numbers, the start layer that restricts the embedding propagation within the subgraph, layer numbers) affect HC-GCN?

4.1 Experimental Settings

Dataset Description. We conduct experiments on Gowalla, Yelp2018, Amazon-book, and Amazon-Kindle Store to evaluate the effectiveness of HC-GCN. All datasets are public and accessible. Gowalla is a dataset from Gowalla [23], where users check in to share their location. Yelp2018 is a dataset that comes from the 2018 revised version of the Yelp Challenge. In Yelp2018, restaurants, bars, and other local businesses are regarded as items. Amazon-book is a dataset in Amazon-Review [24], which is widely used for product recommendations. Table 1 summarizes the statistics of the four datasets. We retain users and services with at least 10 interactions [25] to ensure dataset quality for all datasets.

Table 1. Statistics of the experimental datasets.

Dataset	User #	Item #	Interaction #	Density
Kindle Store	14, 356	15, 885	367, 477	0.00161
Gowalla	29, 858	40, 981	1, 027, 370	0.00084
Yelp2018	31, 668	38, 048	1, 561, 406	0.00130
Amazon-book	52, 643	91, 599	2, 984, 108	0.00062

Evaluation Metrics. In the test set, we consider items that the user did not interact with as negative services. Output the preference score of the user for all services except the positive one in the training set. We use two widely used evaluation protocols to estimate the effectiveness and preference ranking of the top-n recommendations: recall@20 and ndcg@20. What we list are the average metrics of all users in the test set.

Experiment Settings. We implement the HC-GCN model in PyTorch. We fix embedding size to 64, and use the Xavier method [26] to initialize the embedding parameters. HC-GCN chooses Adam [22] to be optimizer, sets a learning rate of 0.001 and all mini-batch size is 2048. The $L2$ regularization coefficient is λ, and its range is $\{1e^{-6}, 1e^{-5}, \ldots, 1e^{-2}\}$, where the optimal value is $1e^{-4}$ for our model. We set the same validation strategies and early stopping as LightGCN. We finally set the number of clusters to 2 and the depth of HC-GCN K to 6. Referring to ablation experiments, we show the results on Gowalla and Kindle Store for space limitation, and omit the results on Yelp2018 and Amazon-book because they show exactly same trend with Gowalla and Kindle Store.

Baselines. To illustrate effectiveness of HC-GCN, we mainly compared it with LightGCN and the following methods:

- MF [2]: This is MF using Bayesian personalized ranking (BPR) loss to optimize parameters. It directly learns interaction between users and services as target value for interaction function.
- GC-MC [17]: It is a model that uses the GCN [15] encoder to learn the representation of users and services. It only uses first-order neighbors. Therefore, we also use only one graph convolutional layer and set the hidden dimension to the embedding size as [17].
- NGCF [6]: This is a model-based CF method using Graph Convolution Network (GCN) [14,15] to refine embeddings. It deepens the graph structure with high-hop neighbors and effectively injects CF signals into the embedding process.
- IMP-GCN [9]: This is a method to design a unsupervised graph generation model to generate a subgraph that can identify the interests of the user, filter out negative information in higher-order neighbors, and effectively alleviate the over-smoothing problem.

4.2 Overall Performance Comparison (RQ1)

Table 2 gives the performance comparison with state-of-the-art methods. HC-GCN gets the best performance on all datasets, demonstrating its effectiveness with clustering to distinguish nodes in higher-order neighbors in the graph convolution operations. Among the baselines LightGCN shows the strongest performance over NGCF by simplifying it with the removal of feature transformation and nonlinear activation. NGCF is better than GC-MC and MF, demonstrating effectiveness of exploring higher-order neighbors of graph structure. GC-MC performs better than MF, which proves GCNs have advantage on learning embedding. The performance of MF indicates that simply conducting inner product between user embedding and service embedding is fail to capture complicated features.

Table 3 gives the performance comparison with IMP-GCN. For IMP-GCN, the subgraph generation model is a three-layer graph neural network, and the

Table 2. Overall performance comparison among our model and competitors. Noticing that the values are reported by percentage with '%' omitted.

Dataset metrics	Gowalla		Yelp2018		Amazon-Book	
	recall	ndcg	recall	ndcg	recall	ndcg
MF	14.74	12.39	5.31	4.50	2.92	2.22
GC-MC	15.14	12.25	5.53	4.67	3.53	2.53
NGCF	15.70	13.27	5.79	4.77	3.44	2.63
LightGCN	**18.30**	**15.54**	**6.49**	**5.30**	**4.11**	**3.15**
HC-GCN	**18.73**	**15.66**	**6.66**	**5.43**	**4.30**	**3.31**
Improv.	2.34%	0.77%	2.61%	2.35%	4.74%	5.08%

model becomes more complex, while Amazon-book is a large dataset, which cannot be calculated when keeping the same embedding dimension on our computer. We choose Kindle Store provided by the IMP-GCN author replaces Amazon-book. Our model is comparable to IMP-GCN in Gowalla and Yelp2018, and even outperforms IMP-GCN in Kindle Store reaching improvement by 4.59%, 3.64% on recall and ndcg. This result indicates effectiveness of the strategy that the user and the service in the deep network structure should maintain their uniqueness by using graph clustering algorithm which partitions all nodes into different subgraphs and each node inside the subgraph belongs to only one of the subgraphs. Meanwhile, the results also show that our strategy can also partition the subgraphs well and keep the model light.

Table 3. Performance comparison between our model and IMP-GCN. Noticing that the values are reported by percentage with '%' omitted.

Dataset metrics	Gowalla		Yelp2018		Kindle Store	
	recall	ndcg	recall	ndcg	recall	ndcg
IMP-GCN	18.45	15.67	6.62	5.45	10.52	6.62
HC-GCN	18.73	15.66	6.66	5.43	11.01	6.86

4.3   Ablation and Effectiveness Analyses (RQ2)

To justify the model, we explore variants of the model here. We first remove the node enhancement, change the number of clusters and the layers where the model starts to perform propagation inside the subgraph. Next, we study the effect of the model when stacking more graph convolutional layers.

Effect of Node Enhancement Technique and Cluster Numbers. Table 4 shows the experimental results of HC-GCN and its variants.

- HC-GCN-node: This variant removes the node enhancement technique (i.e., removing $D^{-\frac{1}{2}}$ and $\bar{D}^{-\frac{1}{2}}$ in (10) and (11)).
- HC-GCN-c_n: This variant denotes HC-GCN with different numbers (i.e., 2, 3, 4) of clusters.

From the experimental results, we can draw some conclusions:

Firstly, node enhancement technique can help our model learn a better embedding, improving the performance. Removing the node enhancement will drop the performance sharply. Secondly, HC-GCN-c_2 achieves a better performance than HC-GCN-c_3 and HC-GCN-c_4 in experiments. This indicates more clusters may filter out too much information including positive information. Although the performance improvement of HC-GCN-c_4 is small, it is better than LightGCN, which shows that our model successfully maintains the uniqueness of users, filters negative information in the graph convolution operation, and alleviates over-smoothing problem.

Table 4. Results comparison between HC-GCN and its variants on Kindle Store and Gowalla. Noticing that the values are reported by percentage with '%' omitted.

Dataset metrics	Kindle Store		Gowalla	
	recall	ndcg	recall	ndcg
LightGCN	10.22	6.24	18.30	15.54
HC-GCN-node	9.78	5.95	17.58	14.71
HG-GCN-c_2	11.00	6.86	18.73	15.63
HG-GCN-c_3	10.97	6.80	18.60	15.53
HG-GCN-c_4	10.87	6.78	18.38	15.39

Effect of Start Layer Restricting Embedding Propagation within the Subgraph. To verify the rationality of the embedding propagation inside the subgraph from the 5th layer, we fix layers K as 6 and set embedding propagation inside the subgraph from the 1st to the 6th order, and the results are shown in Fig. 2. It obviously shows that the case that starts to perform embedding propagation inside the subgraph from the 5th layer outperforms other cases over both datasets. The experiment results clearly show the reasonable design of HC-GCN.

Effect of Layer Numbers. To explore the effectiveness of HC-GCN in a deeper graph structure, we deepen model and make a detailed comparison with Light-GCN. In this experiment, we stacked the layer from 3 to 7 since the HC-GCN is the same as LightGCN in the first four-orders convolution layer except for the node enhancement technique. We draw the results in Fig. 3. From the results, we draw some conclusions.

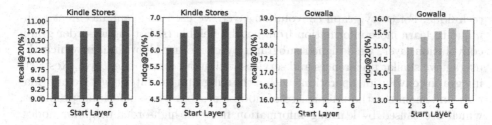

Fig. 2. Results comparison between different start layer restricting embedding propagation within the subgraph on Kindle Store and Gowalla.

First of all, comparing with LightGCN, generally our model performs better than LightGCN stacking 3 or 4 layers. This means that our node enhancement technique improves the performance of the model availably, even in low-order graph convolution operations. Besides, when stacking 3 or 4 layers, LightGCN achieves the best performance, stacking more layers will cause a sharp drop in performance, meaning LightGCN suffers from over-smoothing problem in deeper graph structure. On the contrary, HC-GCN achieves better performance in deeper structure(notice that IMP-GCN verifies that when stacking 6 or 7 layers, a node already aggregates information from almost all the nodes on Kindle Store and Gowalla). The results demonstrate that HC-GCN effectively alleviates the over-smoothing problem. There is a reason to believe that our model can effectively filter negative information and maintain the uniqueness of users and services by clustering graph in higher-order graph convolution operations.

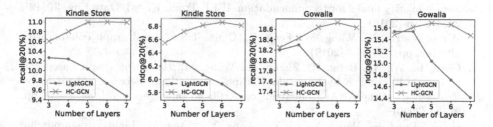

Fig. 3. Results comparison between HC-GCN and LightGCN at different layers on Kindle Store and Gowalla.

5   Conclusion

In our work, we argued that indiscriminately aggregating the information of all neighbor nodes would make dissimilar users more and more similar, making model suffer from over-smoothing problem and learn some negative information. We proposed a new model for service recommendation, that is, HC-GCN, which is composed of two primary components: 1) clustering, 2) node enhancement technique. For every graph convolution layer, we used node enhancement technique to learn more information from nearby neighbors. For higher-order graph convolution layer, we designed subgraph by clustering algorithm, in which the users have similar preferences and services with more common features. Restricting graph convolution operations within the subgraph can filter negative information and maintain the uniqueness of nodes to avoid over-smoothing problems, which are caused by learning information from all high-order neighbor nodes. Comprehensive experiments demonstrate HC-GCN can effectively alleviate the over-smoothing problem and filter noisy information from high-order neighbors in stacking more layers.

References

1. Breese, J.S.: Empirical analysis of predictive algorithms for collaborative filtering. In: Proceedings of the 14th Conference on Uncertainty in Artificial Intelligence, Madison, WI (1998)
2. Koren, Y., Bell, R., Volinsky, C.: Matrix factorization techniques for recommender systems. Computer **42**(8), 30–37 (2009)
3. He, X., Liao, L., Zhang, H., Nie, L., Hu, X., Chua, T.S.: Neural collaborative filtering. In: Proceedings of the 26th International Conference on World Wide Web, pp. 173–182 (2017)
4. Chen, J., Zhang, H., He, X., Nie, L., Liu, W., Chua, T.S.: Attentive collaborative filtering: multimedia recommendation with item-and component-level attention. In: Proceedings of the 40th International ACM SIGIR Conference on Research and Development in Information Retrieval, pp. 335–344 (2017)
5. He, X., He, Z., Song, J., Liu, Z., Jiang, Y.G., Chua, T.S.: Nais: neural attentive item similarity model for recommendation. IEEE Trans. Knowl. Data Eng. **30**(12), 2354–2366 (2018)
6. Wang, X., He, X., Wang, M., Feng, F., Chua, T.S.: Neural graph collaborative filtering, pp. 165–174 (2019)
7. Chen, L., Wu, L., Hong, R., Zhang, K., Wang, M.: Revisiting graph based collaborative filtering: a linear residual graph convolutional network approach. In: Proceedings of the AAAI Conference on Artificial Intelligence, vol. 34, no. 1, pp. 27–34 (2020)
8. He, X., Deng, K., Wang, X., Li, Y., Zhang, Y., Wang, M.: Lightgcn: simplifying and powering graph convolution network for recommendation. In: Proceedings of the 43rd International ACM SIGIR Conference on Research and Development in Information Retrieval, pp. 639–648 (2020)
9. Liu, F., Cheng, Z., Zhu, L., Gao, Z., Nie, L.: Interest-aware message-passing gcn for recommendation. arXiv preprint arXiv:2102.10044 (2021)
10. Karypis, G., Kumar, V.: A fast and high quality multilevel scheme for partitioning irregular graphs. SIAM J. Sci. Comput. **20**(1), 359–392 (1998)
11. Mnih, A., Salakhutdinov, R.R.: Probabilistic matrix factorization. Adv. Neural. Inf. Process. Syst. **20**, 1257–1264 (2007)
12. Koren, Y.: Factorization meets the neighborhood: a multifaceted collaborative filtering model. In: Proceedings of the 14th ACM SIGKDD International Conference on Knowledge Discovery and Data Mining, pp. 426–434 (2008)

13. Yang, J.H., Chen, C.M., Wang, C.J., Tsai, M.F.: Hop-rec: high-order proximity for implicit recommendation. In: Proceedings of the 12th ACM Conference on Recommender Systems, pp. 140–144 (2018)
14. Hamilton, W.L., Ying, R., Leskovec, J.: Inductive representation learning on large graphs. arXiv preprint arXiv:1706.02216 (2017)
15. Kipf, T.N., Welling, M.: Semi-supervised classification with graph convolutional networks. arXiv preprint arXiv:1609.02907 (2016)
16. Bruna, J., Zaremba, W., Szlam, A., LeCun, Y.: Spectral networks and locally connected networks on graphs. arXiv preprint arXiv:1312.6203 (2013)
17. Berg, R.v.d., Kipf, T.N., Welling, M.: Graph convolutional matrix completion. arXiv preprint arXiv:1706.02263 (2017)
18. Ying, R., He, R., Chen, K., Eksombatchai, P., Hamilton, W.L., Leskovec, J.: Graph convolutional neural networks for web-scale recommender systems. In: Proceedings of the 24th ACM SIGKDD International Conference on Knowledge Discovery & Data Mining, pp. 974–983 (2018)
19. Wu, F., Souza, A., Zhang, T., Fifty, C., Yu, T., Weinberger, K.: Simplifying graph convolutional networks. In: International Conference on Machine Learning, PMLR, pp. 6861–6871 (2019)
20. Chiang, W.T., Liu, X., Si, S., Li, Y., Bengio, S., Hsieh, C.J.: Cluster-gcn: an efficient algorithm for training deep and large graph convolutional networks. In: Proceedings of the 25th ACM SIGKDD International Conference on Knowledge Discovery & Data Mining, pp. 257–266 (2019)
21. Rendle, S., Freudenthaler, C., Gantner, Z., Schmidt-Thieme, L.: Bpr: Bayesian personalized ranking from implicit feedback. arXiv preprint arXiv:1205.2618 (2012)
22. Kingma, D., Ba, J.: Adam: a method for stochastic optimization. Comput. Sci. (2014)
23. Liang, D., Charlin, L., Mcinerney, J., Blei, D.M.: Modeling user exposure in recommendation. In: Proceedings of the 25th International Conference (2016)
24. He, R., Mcauley, J.: Ups and downs: modeling the visual evolution of fashion trends with one-class collaborative filtering. In: Proceedings of the International World Wide Web Conferences Steering Committee (2016)
25. He, R., McAuley, J.: Vbpr: visual bayesian personalized ranking from implicit feedback. In: Proceedings of the AAAI Conference on Artificial Intelligence, vol. 30 (2016)
26. Glorot, X., Bengio, Y.: Understanding the difficulty of training deep feedforward neural networks. In: Proceedings of the thirteenth International Conference on Artificial Intelligence and Statistics, JMLR Workshop and Conference Proceedings, pp. 249–256 (2010)

Queueing Theory over OpenvSwitch: Performance Analysis and Optimization

Fuliang Li[1,2], Naigong Zheng[1], Yuchao Zhang[3(✉)], Yishuang Ning[4], and Xingwei Wang[1(✉)]

[1] Northeastern University, Shenyang, People's Republic of China
wangxw@mail.neu.edu.cn
[2] Beijing National Research Center for Information Science and Technology, Beijing, China
[3] Beijing University of Posts and Telecommunications, Beijing, People's Republic of China
yczhang@bupt.edu.cn
[4] Kingdee International Software Group Co., Ltd., Shenzhen, China

Abstract. Software Defined Networking (SDN) offers programmability and flexibility by decoupling the control plane from the data plane. However, its centralized control principle leads to various known performance issues on the data plane, e.g., a mismatch packet on the data plane will ask the control plane how to forward this packet, resulting in extra packet processing delay. In this paper, we take OpenvSwitch (OVS) as an example to investigate the performance of SDN switches based on queueing theory. First, we present the architecture and internal workflow of OVS according to its specifications. Then, we design a queueing network model for OVS. The proposed model is able to evaluate the primary influencing factors on performance, including packet arrival rate, table miss probability, and packet scheduling policy. In addition, we optimize the established model against these influencing factors. We also model the built-in buffer with queueing theory and reveal how buffer size affects performance. Experimental results show that both the proposed optimized model and a reasonable buffer size setting can improve the performance of OVS effectively.

Keywords: Software-defined networking · Queueing theory · Performance analysis · OpenvSwitch

1 Introduction

The control plane is decoupled from the data plane in Software Defined Networks (SDN), providing a logically centralized platform to program the state of the data plane [1]. SDN switches on the data plane are responsible for forwarding data flows according to forwarding rules generated by the control plane. The control plane communicates with the data plane via OpenFlow or OpenFlow-like protocols. SDN could offer differentiated services for different applications

© Springer Nature Switzerland AG 2022
C. Xu et al. (Eds.): ICWS 2021, LNCS 12994, pp. 46–62, 2022.
https://doi.org/10.1007/978-3-030-96140-4_4

and respond to high availability requirements [2]. However, it also faces many performance issues, e.g., packet processing delay is increased due to frequent interactions between the data plane and the control plane.

For the incoming packets of a flow, the switch first lookups the flow table that stores the forwarding rules. If there is a forwarding rule for this flow, the packets forward directly according to the rule matching actions. Otherwise, these mismatch packets will be sent to the controller asking for forwarding decisions by default. The controller decides how to forward these packets and sends operation messages back to the switch. Then the mismatch packets and the subsequent arrival packets of this flow are forwarded. According to the above analysis, it can be seen that packet processing delay includes three parts: 1) forwarding operations in the switch; 2) two-way interactions between the controller and the switch; 3) forwarding decision making in the controller. In this paper, we take OpenvSwitch (OVS) as an example to investigate the performance of SDN from the perspective of model analysis. OVS is a virtual and widely used switch with flexible and programmable ability [3, 4].

Some studies adopt mathematical methodologies to analyze the SDN performance detailedly. Azodolmolky et al. [5] describe functionalities of SDN with a model, which is built based on network calculus. It is the first time that network calculus is utilized to model the behaviors of SDN. Delay and queue length boundaries, as well as the buffer length, are analyzed. Jarschel et al. [6] utilize the feedback orientated queueing theory to evaluate the interactions between the control plane and the data plane. Markovian servers are adopted for SDN, i.e. an M/M/1 for the switch and an M/M/1/m for the controller. The main difference between queuing theory and network calculus is that the former is used to model the performance of a system under a stable state, while the latter calculates the boundaries of a system in the worst cases.

Understanding the performance and limitations of SDN is a crucial issue for real deployment. Existing studies have proved the benefits of mathematical analysis models for the performance analysis of SDN. However, few studies focus on how to improve the performance based on the analysis models. Different from previous studies, we propose a series of models for OVS according to its specifications [7]. We not only reveal how the influencing factors affect the performance with a queueing network model, but also evaluate how to improve the performance based on the optimized models.

To sum up, our main contributions of this paper are summarized as follows.

- We present a queueing network model on the basis of the workflow of OVS. We first divide packet processing into several phases and establish queueing network model at each processing phase. We then evaluate the proposed models across different influencing factors, including packet arrival rate, table miss probability, and packet scheduling policy.
- To reduce the packet processing delay, we optimize the proposed model from many aspects, including multi-threaded processing, priority queue settings, and different packet scheduling policies. We evaluate the optimized models through a comparison analysis.

– To reduce interaction delay between the controller and the switch, we model the built-in buffer based on queueing theory. We interpret how buffer size affects packet processing delay with the built-in buffer model.

The remainder of this paper is organized as follows. Section 2 presents the related studies. Section 3 provides an overview of OVS. Section 4 introduces the queueing network models. Section 5 evaluates the established models with experimental analysis. We conclude the paper in Sect. 6.

2   Related Work

Considering different influencing factors, existing studies have proposed some approaches to evaluate and improve the performance of SDN. Ansell *et al.* [8] present a network performance prediction tool based on queueing analytic models and couple with real-time measurement. It has the ability to examine how the performance is affected by the changes of traffic load and link utilization. Muhizi *et al.* [9] evaluate the performance of SDN with queuing network models, which could observe the changes of packet processing delay under different parameter settings. Shang *et al.* [10] model packet processing delay of SDN switches and controller. They mainly investigate how *packet_in* messages affect the performance. Wang *et al.* [11] evaluate the throughput and delay of the control plane based on queuing theory. How the number of switches, as well as the number of threads, affect throughput and delay is studied. Mahmood *et al.* [12] propose a *Jackson* network, which is used to model the data plane, while the controller is modelled as an M/M/1 queue with an infinite buffer or with a finite buffer. Haiyan *et al.* [13] propose a queueing estimation model and extend it for end-to-end delay analysis. Singh *et al.* [14] use queueing theory to model SDN switches from two aspects, *i.e.*, a shared buffer for both control plane traffic and data plane traffic, and a buffer with two priority queues isolating control plane traffic from data plane traffic. Fahmin *et al.* [15] combine SDN with Network Functional Virtualization (NFV) to cope with performance issues. They aim at modelling SDN with NFV with or without the controller. The M/M/1 queuing model is utilized to evaluate the performance.

As a supplement to previous studies, we first model packet processing of OVS to show how the performance is affected by various influencing factors, and more importantly, we verify how to improve the performance with the optimized models against these influencing factors.

3   Overview of OpenvSwitch

This section describes the architecture and working principles of OVS. OVS is a widely used virtual switch for studying OpenFlow networks [3]. It usually works with a centralized controller, which determines the path of a flow by modifying the flow table inside OVS. When packets of a flow cannot match any rules, *packet_in* messages are sent to the controller to request forwarding decisions. On

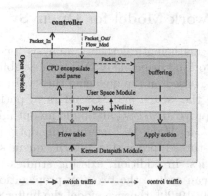

Fig. 1. Internal architecture of OpenvSwitch

the other hand, OVS can also run without the controller. It forwards the packets according to the messages of layer logic. In this paper, we focus on the former case considering the interaction between OVS and the controller.

As depicted in Fig. 1 there are two major components in OVS, *i.e.*, *user space* module and *kernel datapath* module. The *kernel data path* module receives a packet from the network interface. If there are no rules matching this packet, it will be sent to the CPU of *user space* module. The packet header is encapsulated into a *packet_in* message which is sent to the controller. The controller makes forwarding decisions for the mismatched packet according to global network state information. Then the *packet_out* message and the *flow_mod* message are sent to OVS. The *user space* module parses the messages from the controller, forwarding the mismatched packet and updating the flow table at the same time.

OVS is responsible for forwarding packets at the data plane. OpenFlow protocol allows the controller to communicate with OVS, obtaining statistical information of flow table entries, and dynamically adding, updating, deleting flow forwarding rules in the switches. Thus the controller can monitor the state of the whole network. The *user space* module receives flow forwarding rules from the controller, matching the flow table for all the received packets and forwarding them according to matching actions. OVS caches the results in the *kernel data path* module so as to realize fast forwarding of the subsequent arrival packets. It allows OVS to work independently of any SDN controller as it only needs to understand the OpenFlow protocol [4]. Through the above analysis, it can be seen that packet processing delay is mainly composed of the processing delay within OVS (including the flow table lookup delay and the delay of processing *packet_in* message, *packet_out* message, and *flow_mod* message), the two-way propagation delay between the controller and the switch, and the delay of making decisions in the controller.

4   Queueing Network Model for OpenvSwitch

This section presents a mathematical theory analysis for packet processing in OVS. We analyze the working principle of OVS and establish the mathematical model, called *Model SC*, based on the queueing theory. In *Model SC*, "*S*" refers to packet processing in the switch and "*C*" refers to packet processing in the controller. Then, we improve *Model SC* and build an optimized queuing network model, which is called *Model MSC*. "*M*" means using optimized methods to build models, including multi-thread processing, priority queue settings, and different packet scheduling policies. In addition, existing studies have shown that the built-in buffer of OVS can reduce the two-way propagation delay between the controller and the switch [19,20], thus we model the buffer with queueing theory to investigate how buffer size affects the performance.

4.1   Queueing Network Model (*Model SC*) Analysis

We build a queueing network model for OVS and analyze different influencing factors that affect packet processing delay. According to the working principle of OVS, packet processing in OVS is divided into four phases. As depicted in Fig. 2, the switch is built into a queueing network model, i.e., *Model SC*, which can be decomposed into four subsystems, each of which is established as a queueing model. Detailed analysis of each phase is described as follows.

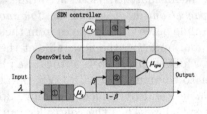

Fig. 2. The queueing network model for OpenvSwitch

Phase One: The Lookup Process Within the Flow Table. We simplify the lookup process of the flow table and establish an M/M/1/K model, where K is the maximum capacity of the input queue of the port. We assume that packet arrivals obey *Poisson* distribution denoted by λ and time of flow table lookup obeys negative exponential distribution with the service rate denoted by μ_s. Due to the limitation of queue capacity, the arrival packets may get lost. The queue capacity is a finite integer [16,17], so the loss probability could be calculated. The loss probability P_s at this phase is illustrated as Eq. (1).

$$P_s = (\frac{\lambda}{\mu_s})^K \tag{1}$$

Where, λ means the average packet arrival rate and μ_s is expressed as the average lookup rate of flow table in the switch.

This phase mainly conducts flow table lookup for the arrival packets. If the packets match forwarding rules, forwarding operations are executed directly. Otherwise, the packets are forwarded to the CPU of *user space* module for further processing. The average processing time of this phase is calculated as Eq. (2) based on queueing theory.

$$d_{i,1} = \frac{1}{\mu_s - (1 - P_s)\lambda} \tag{2}$$

Phase Two: The Encapsulation of *packet_in* Message. If an arrival packet does not match any rules of the flow table, this packet will be forwarded to the CPU of *user space* module. The header of this mismatched packet is extracted and encapsulated into a *packet_in* message which is sent to the controller for forwarding decisions. The probability of such a situation is denoted as the table-miss rate represented by β. Therefore, we consider the process within the CPU as an M/M/1 queueing model, and assume that the average processing time at this phase obeys negative exponential distribution represented by μ_2. In addition, the CPU receives the control operation packets from the controller at the same time. It is assumed that the CPU adopts *First In First Out (FIFO)* strategy for packet processing.

Phase Three: Packet Processing in the Controller. The controller has a global view and formulates forwarding decisions based on network state information. We simplify the process of the controller and mainly focus on the processing of *packet_in* messages. We establish a single queueing model for the controller. We assume that the controller has a queue with an infinite capacity for *packet_in* messages. When a *packet_in* message arrives at the controller, the controller processes it with a *FIFO* queue. The queue in the controller is denoted as an M/M/1 queueing model. Existing studies have already investigated such kinds of models for SDN controllers [12,18]. The average processing delay of a *packet_in* message in the controller can be calculated by Eq. (3).

$$d_{i,3} = \frac{1}{\mu_c - \lambda_c} \tag{3}$$

Where λ_c refers to the average packet arrival rate, and μ_c refers to the average packet processing rate within the controller.

Phase Four: Parsing the Messages from the Controller. After the controller parsing the *packet_in* message, it formulates forwarding decisions and sends a *packet_out* message and a *flow_mod* message to the switch. The *packet_out* message instructs the switch to directly forward the mismatched packet through a specified interface and the *flow_mod* message instructs the switch to install, update or delete the forwarding rule in the flow table. At this phase, the CPU is mainly in charge of parsing the control operation messages from the controller. The packets are forwarded according to the parsing results. It is suited as an M/M/1 model, and the parsing process is assumed to follow the negative exponential distribution. The processing rate is denoted by μ_4.

Since phase two and phase four have roughly the same processing in the switch CPU, we can combine them into a queuing model. Note that the *FIFO* queueing strategy is adopted. Hence the parameters of the queuing model meet the conditions as shown in Eq. (4).

$$\begin{cases} \lambda_{cpu} = \lambda_2 + \lambda_4 \\ \mu_2 + \mu_4 \leq \mu_{cpu} \end{cases} \tag{4}$$

Where μ_{cpu} is the maximum processing capability of the switch CPU. Therefore, the average processing time within the switch CPU is calculated as Eq. (5).

$$d_{i,2} + d_{i,4} = \frac{1}{\mu_2 + \mu_4 - \lambda_{cpu}} \tag{5}$$

We consider propagation delay between the switch and the controller, because it is important to estimate packet processing delay. It consists of constant propagation delay and dynamic queuing delay. In this paper, we analyze the maximum propagation delay between the switch and the controller, *i.e.*, $d_t = \max\limits_{i=1,2,\ldots,n} \{d_{i,t}\}$.

In a real network, there is almost no queuing in the propagating process [13], so the queuing delay can be ignored. The maximum propagation delay between the switch and the controller can be considered a constant as shown in Eq. (6).

$$d_t = \max\limits_{i=1,2,\ldots,n} \{d_{i,t}\} = constant \tag{6}$$

According to the queuing network models established above, we can estimate the processing delay of a packet, from arriving at the switch to being forwarded to the next hop successfully. The average packet processing delay D_{pkt} mainly consists of four parts which are described as Eq. (7).

$$D_{pkt} = \frac{1}{n} \sum_{i=1}^{n} [(1 - \beta)d_{i,1} + \beta(\sum_{k=1}^{4} d_{i,k} + 2d_t)] \tag{7}$$

Where $d_{i,k}$ is the processing delay of the i_{th} packet at phase k.

4.2   Optimized Queueing Network Model (*Model MSC*) analysis

To reduce packet processing delay, an optimized queueing model for OVS is proposed, i.e., *Model MSC*. Compared with *Model SC*, *Model MSC* mainly optimize flow table lookup and switch CPU processing with the methods of multi-threaded processing, priority queue settings, and different queue scheduling policies. The optimized queueing network model is shown in Fig. 3.

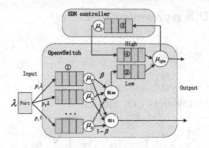

Fig. 3. The optimized queueing network model for OpenvSwitch

Optimizing Flow Table Lookup. To reduce the delay of flow table lookup, we use multi-threaded processing to achieve rapid flow table lookup at phase one. The switch CPU uses *FIFO* strategy to process packets. We define the queueing network model as *Model MSC-F* and "*F*" means the *FIFO* queue is utilized.

During the multi-thread process, each thread is established as an M/M/1/K model, so the multi-thread process can be regarded as an M/M/C/K queuing network model. When packets arrive at the switch, they will be assigned a thread with the probability p_j meeting $\sum_{j=1}^{c} p_j = 1$. The probability each thread receiving packets follows the proportional relation of $\{p_1, p_2, ..., p_c\}$. The average processing delay of multi-thread process is depicted in Eq. (8).

$$d'_{i.1} = \max_{j=1,2,...,m} \{ \frac{1}{\mu_s - (1 - P_s)p_j\lambda} \} \tag{8}$$

To further optimize the performance, we can use different scheduling policies to assign the arrival packets during the multi-thread processing. We conduct a comparison analysis about this point in Sect. 5.

Optimizing Switch CPU Processing. We set the priority queues in the switch CPU, handling messages from the controller as quickly as possible to reduce the waiting delay of the packets buffered in the built-in buffer. Figure 3 shows the model which uses priority queues for the switch CPU with finite capacity. We define this model as *Model MSC-P* and "*P*" refers to the priority queues designed in the switch CPU.

Priority queues isolate control packets from data packets. In *Model MSC-P*, packets received at phase two enter into the low-priority queue and packets received at phase four (*i.e.*, *packet_out* messages and *flow_mod* messages) enter into the high-priority queue. The switch CPU can be regarded as the server of a queuing system. It prioritizes the packets in the high-priority queue. When there are no packets in the high-priority queue, it processes the packets in the low-priority queue. Therefore, the control packet arrival rate can be considered as the average packet arrival rate of switch CPU (i.e., $\lambda'_{cpu,}$). The average processing delay of the switch CPU is represented by Eq. (9).

$$d'_{i,2} + d'_{i,4} = \frac{1}{\mu_{cpu} - \lambda'_{cpu}} \tag{9}$$

Based on the above analysis, we can calculate the average processing delay with the optimized queueing network model.

$$D'_{pkt} = \frac{1}{n} \sum_{i=1}^{n} [(1 - \beta)d'_{i,1} + \beta(\sum_{k=1}^{4} d'_{i,k} + 2d_t)] \tag{10}$$

Where $d'_{i,k}$ is the processing delay of the i_{th} packet at phase k in *Model MSC*.

4.3   Built-in Buffer Queueing Model Analysis

The main purpose of setting up a built-in buffer is to store mismatched packets. It caches subsequent packets belonging to the same flow in the built-in buffer, which can reduce the number of *packet_in* messages and decrease the communication load between the controller and the switch. Generally, there are three main situations that need to be handled by the buffer.

(1) When receiving a mismatched packet, it is necessary to find out whether there are packets belonging to the same flow in the built-in buffer. If there are, the mismatched packet will be stored in the buffer. Otherwise, its header information will be encapsulated into a *packet_in* message and the message will be sent to the controller.
(2) When waiting for the controller to return the *packet_out* message, if a packet stored in the built-in buffer exceeds the time limit, proper processing is required. For example, the switch sends a *packet_in* message to the controller again or directly discards this packet.
(3) The controller makes a forwarding decision for the packets of a flow and generates a *packet_out* message sent to the switch. The switch parses the *packet_out* message and forwards the buffered packets of this flow to a specific interface according to the forwarding operation.

Existing studies apply the built-in buffer to reduce the interactions between the controller and the switch [19,20]. When using the flow-level buffering mechanism [19], only one *packet_in* message will be sent to the controller for all the mismatched packets of a flow. Experiment results show that the built-in buffer can reduce the packet processing delay effectively. In this paper, we model the built-in buffer based on queueing theory to investigate how buffer size affects the packet processing delay through a theoretical analysis.

We establish a triggered queueing network according to the processing mechanism of the built-in buffer. As shown in Fig. 4, the process within the controller is simplified to an M/M/1 queueing model. The *packet_out* message from the controller is considered as the trigger information to release corresponding packets buffered in the built-in buffer.

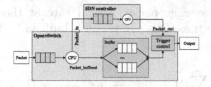

Fig. 4. The built-in buffer queueing model

In this model, we assume that the arrival process of mismatched packets follows *Poisson* distribution with the parameter of λ_{mis}. The average rate of packet arriving at the controller satisfies Eq. (11).

$$\lambda_{buf} = \omega \lambda_{mis} \tag{11}$$

Where ω denotes the proportion of *packet_in* messages generated for arrival packets.

The processing process of the controller obeys the negative exponential distribution with the parameter of μ_{buf}. The average processing delay of the controller can be calculated by Eq. (12).

$$d_{buf} = \frac{1}{\mu_{buf} - \lambda_{buf}} \tag{12}$$

The propagation delay of the communication channel between the switch and the controller is considered invariable. As shown in Eq. (13), the maximum propagation delay is adopted.

$$d_{s \to c} = d_{c \to s} = d_t \tag{13}$$

Where $d_{s \to c}$ denotes the delay between the switch sending the *packet_in* message and the controller receiving the *packet_in* message, and $d_{c \to s}$ denotes the delay between the controller sending the *packet_out* message and the switch receiving the *packet_out* message.

If there are no rules matching the packets of a flow, a series of operations are carried out for setting up this flow. The delay of setting up a flow starts from the first packet of the flow entering the switch to the packet leaving the switch. According to the above analysis, the delay of setting up a flow can be calculated as Eq. (14).

$$D_{buf} = d_{s \to c} + d_{buf} + d_{c \to s} = 2d_t + \frac{1}{\mu_{buf} - \lambda_{buf}} \tag{14}$$

The built-in buffer size depends on the number of arrival packets during the period of setting up flows. Hence the size of the built-in buffer is expressed as Eq. (15).

$$B = \lambda_{pkt\_buf} D_{buf} \tag{15}$$

Where λ_{pkt_buf} is the average packet arrival rate at the built-in buffer. The packet processing delay (i.e., D_{pkt_buf}) with a built-in buffer can be calculated by Eq. (16).

$$D_{pkt\_buf} = \frac{1}{n} \sum_{i=1}^{n} [(1 - \beta)d'_{i,1} + \beta(d'_{i,CPU} + D_{buf} + \frac{B}{\lambda_{release}})] \qquad (16)$$

Where $d'_{i,CPU}$ denotes the packet processing delay of switch CPU and $\lambda_{release}$ denotes the average rate of releasing the packets cached in the built-in buffer.

5   Performance Evaluation

In this paper, a switch interacting with a controller is taken as the experimental scenario. The proposed queuing network models are carried out based on discrete event system simulation. We conduct a theoretical analysis of the performance influencing factors, including average packet arrival rate, flow table miss rate, packet scheduling policy, and built-in buffer size.

The parameter settings for the proposed queueing network models are shown in Table 1 [9,11]. The average packet arrival rate λ ranges from 1000 to 4000 pkts/s and the flow table miss rate β ranges from 0.1 to 1. The flow table lookup rate μ_s is 2500 pkts/s and the switch CPU processing rate μ_{cpu} is 2000 pkts/s. The controller processing rate μ_c is 2500 pkts/s and the packet loss rate P_s ranges from 0.01 to 0.1. Each experiment is executed 20 times under different parameter settings. The average packet processing delay and the packet loss rate are calculated. How the influencing factors affect the performance is investigated with these analytical models, including *Model SC* which is the standard queueing network model for OVS, *Model MSC-F* which optimizes flow table lookup, and *Model MSC-P* which optimizes switch CPU processing.

Table 1. Parameter settings for the proposed queuing network models

Parameters	value
Table miss probability, β	0.1–1
Packet arrival rate, λ	1000–4000 pkts/s
Lookup processing rate, μ_s	2500 pkts/s
Switch CPU processing rate, μ_{cpu}	2000 pkts/s
Controller processing rate, μ_c	2500 pkts/s
Packet loss rate, P_s	0.01–0.1

5.1   Impact of Packet Arrival Rate

Packet arrival rates may have a significant impact on the processing delay. Figure 5a shows the impact of arrival rates on average packet processing delay D_{pkt} of *Model SC*, *Model MSC-F* and *Model MSC-P*. For *Model SC*, packet arrival rate affects the average processing delay greatly, and the value of D_{pkt} increases rapidly with the growth of λ. This is because the number of packets arriving at the switch increases with the increase of λ, resulting in a longer waiting time in the input queue.

Compared to *Model SC*, the average processing delay of *Model MSC-P* and *Model MSC-F* is less affected by the packet arrival rate. This is because multi-thread processing can accelerate packet processing and reduce the input queuing delay. At the same time, *Model MSC-P* prioritizes the decision messages from the controller, which reduces the waiting delay of mismatched packets. Therefore, the average packet processing delay of *Model MSC-P* is smaller than that of *Model MSC-P*. We also find that *Model MSC-P* is basically not affected by the packet arrival rate.

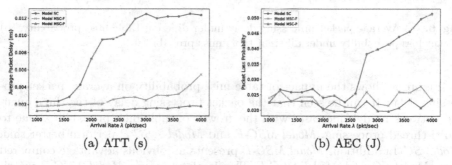

(a) ATT (s)   (b) AEC (J)

Fig. 5. (a) Average packet processing delay under different arrival rates, (b) Packet loss probability under different arrival rates.

Figure 5b shows the impact of arrival rates on packet loss probability, i.e., P_s. It can be observed that *Model MSC-P* and *Model MSC-F* have better performance on packet loss probability. P_s of *Model MSC-P* is smaller than that of *Model MSC-F* in most cases. Compared to *Model SC*, the packet loss probability of *Model MSC-P* and *Model MSC-F* is less affected by λ. This is attributed to the multi-thread processing mechanism and the priority queue in the optimized models. *Model SC* adopts the single-thread processing mechanism to process packets. When λ is not greater than μ_s, packet loss probability is low and fluctuates around 2.5%. This is because packets are processed quickly by the switch and there is no congestion. When λ is greater than μ_s, congestion occurs in the switch, making the packet loss probability increase. After that threshold, P_s of *Model SC* increases with the growth of λ.

5.2   Impact of Table Miss Probability

Table miss rate β is the ratio of mismatched packets to the total arrival packets. It is expressed by Eq. (17).

$$\beta = \frac{N_{pkt\_in}}{N_{total}} \tag{17}$$

Where N_{pkt_in} means the number of mismatch packets and N_{total} means the number of total arrival packets.

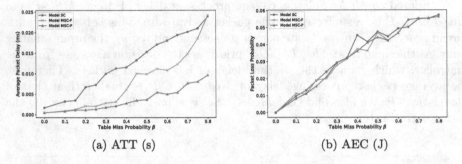

(a) ATT (s)   (b) AEC (J)

Fig. 6. (a) Average packet processing delay under different table miss probability, (b) Packet loss probability under different table miss probability β.

Figure 6a shows the impact of table miss probability on average packet processing delay. It can be seen that the packet processing delay of the three queuing network models increases with the growth of table miss probability. Due to multi-thread processing, *Model MSC-F* and *Model MSC-P* perform better than *Model SC*. In addition, *Model MSC-P* presents an obvious advantage compared with *Model SC* and *Model MSC-F*. This is also because *Model MSC-P* prioritizes the control messages from the controller and forwards the packets cached in the built-in buffer of the switch as soon as possible, which greatly reduces the waiting delay of mismatched packets. Therefore, *Model MSC-P* can effectively mitigate the impact of table miss probability on packet processing delay.

Figure 6b shows the changes of packet loss under different table miss probability. It can be seen that the packet loss rates of the three models increase with the growth of table miss probability. The values of them are similar to each other under the same flow table miss probability. That is to say *Model MSC-F* and *Model MSC-P* can not effectively reduce the packet loss. To sum up, when the table miss rate is high, *Model MSC-P* has smaller packet processing delay and lower packet loss rate. In other words, it performs better in handling the mismatched packets.

5.3   Impact of Packet Scheduling Policies

For the optimized models, the switch adopts the multi-thread processing mechanism to process the received packets. Each thread contains a *FIFO* queue with limited capacity. How to schedule the arrival packets for the parallel queues is worth discussing. In this section, we evaluate the impact of packet scheduling policies on processing delay. The following four packet scheduling policies are designed for the multi-thread processing mechanism of *Model MSC-F*.

Policy One. When a packet arrives at the switch, the processing unit schedules the first input queue to process it. If this input queue is blocked by this packet, the processing unit will allocate subsequent packets to another queue. If the input queues of all threads are blocked, the processing unit will no longer receive packets for the switch.

Policy Two. The processing unit allocates arrival packets to input queues in turn for processing. The processing unit will schedule from queue one to queue M assuming that the interface has M queues in total. After polling M queues, the processing unit schedules from queue one.

Policy Three. Packets are allocated to input queues of multiple threads according to a specified probability. An arrival packet will be assigned to a queue of one thread with the probability p_j, where $\sum_{j=1}^{c} p_j = 1$. The probability assigned to each thread follows a proportional relationship, i.e., $\{p_1, p_2, ..., p_c\}$. The processing unit distributes the arrival packets to the threads for processing according to the proportional relationship.

Policy Four. When a packet arrives at the switch, the processing unit randomly assigns it to an input queue for processing. The input queue of each thread is equally to be selected.

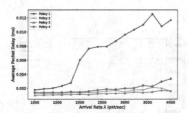

Fig. 7. Average packet processing delay of different scheduling policies

Figure 7 shows the impact of packet scheduling policies on processing delay across different arrival rates. Results show that the packet processing delay of policy one increases with the growth of the arrival rate. When $\lambda \leq \mu_s$, the average packet processing delay is low and keeps stable. When $\lambda > \mu_s$, the packet arrival rate exceeds the switch processing rate. As a result, the average packet processing delay presents a rapid growth with the increase of arrival rate. Packet processing delay of the other three policies is not significantly affected by the arrival rate. Switch randomly assigns packets to threads, which can alleviate the congestion effectively. It can be seen that policy three has the lowest processing delay in most cases. This is because the switch distributes packets to threads according to the pre-defined probability relationship. This makes full use of multi-thread resources, which can reduce the processing delay of the switch.

5.4   Impact of Built-in Buffer Size

Built-in buffer is mainly used to store mismatched packets. When the switch receives the first data packet of a new flow, the switch CPU encapsulates the header information of the packet and sends a *packet_in* message to the controller, while the subsequent arrival packets of this flow will be buffered in the built-in buffer, waiting for the decision issued by the controller. When the built-in buffer is exhausted, the switch CPU will encapsulate the whole mismatched packet into *packet_in* message and send it to the controller. After making a decision, the controller will generate *packet_out* message and *flow_mod* message, which are sent to the switch. This will lead to an increase in the load of the communication channel between the switch and the controller, resulting in a rapid decline in the processing performance of the switch. Therefore, avoiding the exhaustion of the built-in buffer is the key to reduce the switch processing delay. Hence it is necessary to determine the size of the built-in buffer to reduce its impact on the processing delay.

By setting different built-in buffer sizes and carrying out several experiments under different packet arrival rates, we investigate the changes of processing delay and then determine the range of the built-in buffer size. Since the size of packets arriving at the switch may be different, a fixed storage space is allocated for each buffered packet in order to store mismatched packets conveniently. Figure 8 shows the packet processing delay of different flows across different built-in buffer sizes.

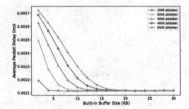

Fig. 8. Flow setup delay

It can be seen that the average processing delay decreases obviously with the increase of the buffer size. However, when buffer size exceeds a certain value, its impact on packet processing delay becomes smaller until it remains basically unchanged. In addition, the impact of arrival rate on processing delay decreases with the increase of the buffer size. When the size of the built-in buffer is constant, the processing delay increases with the growth of arrival rate. However, when the buffer size exceeds 20 KB, the processing delay will no longer be affected by the arrival rate. Therefore, the built-in buffer of the switch can alleviate the impact of arrival rate on processing delay to a certain extent. Therefore, we can set the built-in buffer size for the switch according to the experiment results, so as to reduce the processing delay of the switch and improve the performance of the whole network.

6   Conclusion

In this paper, we investigate and optimize the performance of OpenvSwitch with queueing theory. First, we present a basic queueing network model according to the working principles of OVS. And then we evaluate the performance influencing factors with the proposed model. In addition, we optimize the basic model from many aspects, including multi-threaded processing, setting priority queues, and utilizing different packet scheduling policies. Finally, we expound the impact of the built-in buffer size on packet processing delay.

We evaluate these optimized methods through a comparison analysis. We compare the performance of *Model SC* (basic model), *Model MSC-F* (multi-thread with the *FIFO* queue model) and *Model MSC-P* (multi-thread with the priority queue model). Results reveal that the optimized models have better performance than the basic model. We also find that the built-in buffer size has a more significant impact on packet processing delay via theoretical verification. In the future, we will extend the use of the mathematical analysis model to evaluate and optimize the performance of SDN switches and provide guidelines for optimal switch design.

Acknowledgements. The authors would like to thank Dr. Qing Li for his kind help and constructive comments. This work is supported by the National Key Research and Development Program of China under Grant No. 2019YFB1802600; the National Natural Science Foundation of China under Grant No. 62072091; the Fundamental Research Funds for the Central Universities under Grant No. N2016005; Shenzhen Development and Reform Commission No. XMHT20200105010; Beijing Natural Science Foundation under Grant No. M21030; Open Research Fund Program of Beijing National Research Center for Information Science and Technology.

References

1. Xia, W., Wen, Y., Foh, C.H., Niyato, D., Xie, H.: A survey on software-defined networking. IEEE Commun. Surv. Tutor. **17**(1), 27–51 (2015)
2. Benzekki, K., Fergougui, A.E., Elalaoui, A.E.: Software defined networking (SDN): a survey. Secur. Commun. Netw. **9**(18), 5803–5833 (2016)
3. OVS, Open vSwitch manual. http://www.openvswitch.org/. Accessed 16 May 2017

4. Pfaff, B., et al.: The design and implementation of open vSwitch. In: 12th USENIX Symposium on Networked Systems Design and Implementation (NSDI 2015), Oakland, CA, pp. 117–130 (2015)
5. Azodolmolky, S., Nejabati, R., Pazouki, M., Wieder, P., Yahyapour, R., Simeonidou, D.: An analytical model for software defined networking: a network calculus-based approach. In: IEEE Global Communications Conference (GLOBECOM), Atlanta, GA, 1397–1402 (2013)
6. Jarschel, M., Oechsner, S., Schlosser, D., Pries, R., Goll, S., Tran-Gia, P.: Modeling and performance evaluation of an OpenFlow architecture. In: 23rd International Teletraffic Congress (ITC), San Francisco, CA, pp. 1–7 (2011)
7. OpenFlow Switch Specification. https://www.opennetworking.org/. Accessed 20 June 2018
8. Ansell, J., Seah, W.K.G., Ng, B., et al.: Making queueing theory more palatable to SDN/OpenFlow-based network practitioners. In: Network Operations and Management Symposium, pp. 1119–1124. IEEE (2016)
9. Muhizi, S., Shamshin, G., Muthanna, A., Kirichek, R., Vladyko, A., Koucheryavy, A.: Analysis and performance evaluation of SDN queue model. In: Koucheryavy, Y., Mamatas, L., Matta, I., Ometov, A., Papadimitriou, P. (eds.) WWIC 2017. LNCS, vol. 10372, pp. 26–37. Springer, Cham (2017). https://doi.org/10.1007/978-3-319-61382-6_3
10. Shang, Z., Wolter, K.: Delay evaluation of OpenFlow network based on queueing model. arXiv preprint arXiv:1608.06491 (2016)
11. Wang, Z., Zhao, S., Fan, Z., Wan, X.: Performance modeling and analysis of control plane for SDN based on queuing theory. Wirel. Pers. Commun. 1–11 (2017)
12. Mahmood, K., Chilwan, A., Sterb, O., Jarschel, M.: Modelling of OpenFlow-based software-defined networks: the multiple node case. IET Netw. 4(5), 278–284 (2015)
13. Haiyan, M., Jinyao, Y., Georgopoulos, P., Plattner, B.: Towards SDN based queuing delay estimation. China Commun. 13(3), 27–36 (2016)
14. Singh, D., Ng, B., Lai, Y.C., et al.: Modelling software-defined networking: switch design with finite buffer and priority queueing. In: IEEE Conference on Local Computer Networks, pp. 567–570. IEEE Computer Society (2017)
15. Fahmin, A., Lai, Y.C., Hossain, M.S., Lin, Y.D., Saha, D.: Performance modeling of SDN with NFV under or aside the controller. In: 2017 5th International Conference on Future Internet of Things and Cloud Workshops (FiCloudW), Prague, pp. 211–216 (2017)
16. Simcoe, R.J., Robert, J.P.: Perspectives on ATM switch architecture and the influence of traffic pattern assumptions on switch design. ACM SIGCOMM Comput. Commun. Rev. 25(2), 93–105 (1995)
17. Liew, S.C.: Performance of various input-buffered and output-buffered ATM switch design principles under bursty traffic: simulation study. IEEE Trans. Commun. 42(234), 1371–1379 (1994)
18. Wang, G., Li, J., Chang, X.: Modeling and performance analysis of the multiple controllers' approach in software defined networking. In: 2015 IEEE 23rd International Symposium on Quality of Service (IWQoS), Portland, OR, pp. 73–74 (2015)
19. Li, F., Cao, J., Wang, X., et al.: Applying buffer to SDN switches: benefits analysis and mechanism design. IEEE Trans. Cloud Comput. 9, 54–65 (2018)
20. Li, F., Cao, J., Wang, X., Sun, Y., Pan, T., Liu, X.: Adopting SDN switch buffer: benefits analysis and mechanism design. In: IEEE International Conference on Distributed Computing Systems, pp. 2171–2176. IEEE (2017)

Linked Data Quality Assessment: A Survey

Aparna Nayak(✉) , Bojan Božić , and Luca Longo

SFI Centre for Research Training in Machine Learning, School of Computer Science,
Technological University Dublin, Dublin, Republic of Ireland
{aparna.nayak,bojan.bozic,luca.longo}@tudublin.ie

Abstract. Data is of high quality if it is fit for its intended use in operations, decision-making, and planning. There is a colossal amount of linked data available on the web. However, it is difficult to understand how well the linked data fits into the modeling tasks due to the defects present in the data. Faults emerged in the linked data, spreading far and wide, affecting all the services designed for it. Addressing linked data quality deficiencies requires identifying quality problems, quality assessment, and the refinement of data to improve its quality. This study aims to identify existing end-to-end frameworks for quality assessment and improvement of data quality. One important finding is that most of the work deals with only one aspect rather than a combined approach. Another finding is that most of the framework aims at solving problems related to DBpedia. Therefore, a standard scalable system is required that integrates the identification of quality issues, the evaluation, and the improvement of the linked data quality. This survey contributes to understanding the state of the art of data quality evaluation and data quality improvement. A solution based on ontology is also proposed to build an end-to-end system that analyzes quality violations' root causes.

Keywords: Data quality · Knowledge graphs · Linked data · Quality assessment · Quality improvement

1 Introduction

Data quality is often defined as "fitness for use" which signifies the term data quality is relative [6]. Thus, data with certain quality considered good for one use may not possess sufficient quality for another use. A massive amount of data is available in the public domain in the form of text, tables and linked data. However, most of these data are often incorrect, incomplete or ambiguous.

The term "Knowledge graph" refers to a set of best practices for publishing and connecting linked data on the web following Semantic Web principles. The main goal of Semantic Web is data interoperability, which allows data to be read and understandable both by humans and machine. A large number of published datasets (or sources) that follow linked data principles is currently

© Springer Nature Switzerland AG 2022
C. Xu et al. (Eds.): ICWS 2021, LNCS 12994, pp. 63–76, 2022.
https://doi.org/10.1007/978-3-030-96140-4_5

available and this number grows rapidly. Knowledge graph have a wide range of applications, including recommendation systems [23], semantic search based on entities and relationships, natural language disambiguation, deep reasoning, machine reading, entity consolidation for big data, and text analysis [8]. The semantic richness of knowledge graph can benefit explainable artificial intelligence, an emerging field of machine learning. However, large knowledge graphs such as DBpedia[1] and Wikidata[2] still suffer from different quality problems [21].

Data quality is being one of the major concern this paper aims to achieve the following objectives:

O1: Identification and survey existing data quality assessment/improvement framework/tools and data quality metrics.
O2: Investigate frameworks and tools that enable the quality assessment of data at A-box level.

Our contributions in this paper include identifying various ways to assess and improve problems associated with data quality. A preliminary framework that enables end-to-end systems for data assessment and improvement is also discussed. The rest of this paper is organized as follows. Section 2 discusses the literature present in data quality assessment and improvement. Section 3 provides an outlook for further research. Finally, Sect. 4 concludes the work.

2   Methods for Data Quality Assessment and Improvement

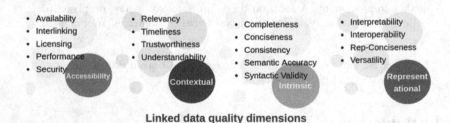

- Availability
- Interlinking
- Licensing
- Performance
- Security

Accessibility

- Relevancy
- Timeliness
- Trustworthiness
- Understandability

Contextual

- Completeness
- Conciseness
- Consistency
- Semantic Accuracy
- Syntactic Validity

Intrinsic

- Interpretability
- Interoperability
- Rep-Conciseness
- Versatility

Representational

Linked data quality dimensions

Fig. 1. Linked data quality dimensions

The objective of the data quality assessment activity is to analyze the relevance of a dataset to its consumers and to help publish better quality data. Analysts working with linked data must assess quality at various levels such as instance, schema and property. Data quality is a multidimensional concept. Various studies have classified data quality metrics into four dimensions intrinsic, accessible,

---

[1] https://wiki.dbpedia.org/.
[2] https://www.wikidata.org/wiki/Wikidata:Main_Page.

representational, and contextual [44] as shown in Fig. 1. Data quality metrics that belong to intrinsic dimensions focus on whether the information correctly and completely represents the real world and whether the information is logically consistent in itself. The accessible dimension encompasses the aspects of data access, authentication, and retrieval in order to retrieve all or a portion of the data required for a particular use case. Representational dimensions capture information about the data's design. Contextual dimensions are those that are highly context-dependent, such as relevance, trustworthiness, comprehendibility, and timeliness. Zaveri et al. [51] discusses a comprehensive survey that includes multiple metrics for evaluating each dimension. It examines 68 quality metrics for linked data and provides a detailed explanation of how each metric is calculated. On the other hand, data quality metrics are divided into baseline and derived by incorporating the metrics defined in Zaveri et al. [51] and ISO 25012[3].

The most frequently encountered issues such as missing data, missing entity relationships, and erroneous data values have a direct impact on data quality. Additionally, converting data from one format to linked data may degrade data quality due to various problems such as errors introduced at the source, parsing values, interpreting, and converting units [48]. Integration of data from multiple sources does not always result data quality improvement; rather, if the sources contain contradictory information, the quality may deteriorate [31]. Regardless of the total number of integrated data sources, quality issues persist at the schema and instance levels [39]. In the following subsections various methods to assess and improve the data quality are discussed.

2.1 Ontologies Based on Data Quality

This section discusses the ontologies that have been modeled in order to identify data quality issues and generate a report on data quality. Data Quality Management (DQM) vocabulary, conceptualizes data quality requirements by focusing on the intrinsic quality of the data [20]. This ontology aids in the description of data quality assessment results and data cleaning rules in a Semantic Web architecture. Data Cleaning Ontology (DCO), one more ontology that represents the data cleaning process [4]. DCO is an advanced version of DQM that assists domain experts with data cleaning. However, these ontologies do not directly help to assess data quality. Data Quality Vocabulary (daQ), helps to represent results of data quality assessment in machine-readable format [15]. This ontology defines a core vocabulary that enables the uniform definition of specific data quality metrics, which data publishers can include in their metadata. W3 has published Data Quality Vocabulary (DQV) [3] to represent data quality assessment in Semantic Web format[4]. Data publisher or consumer can use this vocabulary to represent their data quality assessment report. Fuzzy Quality Data Vocabulary (FQV) extends DQV to represent the fuzzy concepts. Fuzzy

---

[3] https://iso25000.com/index.php/en/iso-25000-standards/iso-25012.

[4] https://www.w3.org/TR/vocab-dqv/.

ontology assesses the data quality using fuzzy inference systems based on user-defined fuzzy rules [5]. The aforementioned ontologies do not help to assess the quality of the data, rather publish quality reports in a machine-readable manner. Data quality is assessed at various levels such as perception, data, processed and, rules. This helps to differentiate validation report of the data quality from the different point of view [35]. Reasoning Violations Ontology (RVO) is an ontology used to validate the triples and reason out the violations if any [9].

Table 1. Ontologies based on data quality

Ontology	Richness	Dataset	Evaluation method
DQM	64	Synthetic data	SPARQL queries
FQV	13	Peel, DBLP (L3S), DBPedia, EIONET	Compared proposed method with Sieve [31]
DQV	10	–	–
RVO	14	Dacura schema manager	Integrated RVO in multiple ontology to identify errors
Grounding based ontology	4	OpenStreetMap data	Domain experts and external dataset such as Google maps

Table 1 compares various ontologies that focus on data quality. Richness of the ontology is computed based on total number of classes in the ontology. Dataset column indicates the dataset used to validate the ontology and evaluation method depicts how the ontology is evaluated.

2.2 Data Quality Assessment

Existing data quality assessment tools differ on various characteristics such as the number of metrics to assess quality, approaches to process data, type of data used to evaluate, user flexibility to choose metric & corresponding weight and assessment report. Luzzu [16] is a stream-oriented data quality assessment framework that requires domain experts to explicitly mention the metrics using either a programming language or declarative statements. Semquire [27], a software tool for linked data quality assessment, implements the quality metrics mentioned in [51] based on user/application requirement. Despite that the framework provides a cyclical process to define quality metrics and evaluate a dataset, it does not address the defects' root causes. A number of other data quality assessment tools focus on either a specific data set or a specific metric mentioned in Table 2.

A plethora of research focus primarily on various levels of linked data. These levels include schema, instance and properties. One of the sources for linked data is (Semi-) structured data. The mapping languages used to convert semi-structured data into linked format impacts the data quality due to incorrect usage of schema in the mapping definitions, mistakes in the original data source [18,41]. Various quality deficiencies at schema and instance level and resolution strategy have been listed in [7]. One more method to assess the data quality is to use of external sources. All RDF triples are compared with external sources to identify inaccurate information present in the knowledge graph [29]. The correctness of RDF triples can be measured by a confidence score that is generated based on the reliability score of each triple. Other works analyze the quality of DBpedia available in different language editions such as Spanish [34], and Arabic [26] by comparing different versions of DBpedia or comparing various language editions. The results of the research can be used by the DBpedia community (publisher) to eliminate the errors in its further editions.

Table 2. Data quality assessment tools

Tool	Data source	Goal	Evaluation method
Sieve [31]	DBpedia	Identify the quality and integrate data from multiple sources to get improved data set	Not mentioned
TripleCheck Mate [25]	DBpedia	Assess and improve DBpedia data	Crowdsourcing
Databugger [24]	DBpedia	Test driven data debugging framework based on SPARQL queries	Used same queries against 5 different data set to show case the tool re-usability
Luzzu [16]	Real world dataset	To identify the quality of the linked dataset	Evaluated the tool for scalability
LD Sniffer [32]	DBpedia	To analyze the availability of the given URI and assess the retrieved data using LDQM	Not mentioned
Semquire [27]	Real world dataset	To identify the quality of given linked dataset	Compared various publicly available KG

Data quality assessment tools such as ABSTAT [36], Loupe [33], DistQualityAssessment [42], Roomba [2] focus on understanding statistical information which include number of triples, and implicit vocabulary information. The information derived from these tools help the user get insight into the dataset that includes detecting outliers in the vocabulary usage, most frequent patterns in linked data, and thus interpreting data quality. Data quality framework KBQ [40,43] help in evolution analysis of linked data by comparing all the triples of two consecutive releases of the dataset. Other related work [18,47] assess the data quality; however, it fails to mention any technique to improve the identified data quality problem. In addition, some methods involve manual work to evaluate each fact for correctness [1,50].

2.3 Data Quality Improvement

Data quality improvement can make use of either external data or the knowledge graph itself. The presence of illegal values, typographical errors and missing information may lead to poor data quality [39]. Knowledge graph refinement [37], and reasoning is a technique used to refine existing data and add missing hidden information. Reasoning methods are based on logical rules, neural networks, and continuous vector space that can be used to infer missing knowledge by refining the given knowledge graph [12]. Sieve [31] compares two different data sources and chooses the accurate value based on time-closeness and preference. Sieve is a data fusion approach that enriches the DBpedia data by comparing English and Portuguese wikipedia editions. Conceptnet, one of the publicly available knowledge graph is improved by adding more triples that are extracted from news and tweets [49]. Though the accuracy of the relation extraction model is low, authors haven't mentioned anything about the quality of the added information.

Quality of the data can be improved by using supervised methods [10,11,30], or unsupervised methods [17,38,45]. Data quality can improve by resolving range violation [28], outlier detection [17], tensor factorization [45] and link prediction [10,11,30]. Statistical relational learning plays a significant role in knowledge graph as it also studies the graph structure of knowledge graph [22].

2.4 Root Cause Identification

Data contains errors that need to be identified and resolved. Identification of the location of the data quality problem is possible by root cause analysis. Various datasets published by the government have been evaluated for quality defects such as missing data, format issues, logical duplication and many more. Some of the common mistakes that is often generated by publisher side that affect quality problems and suggestions to improve the same are listed by [13]. However, they have not mentioned the fine-grained level of quality analysis. In another related study, [46] root causes of data quality violations are identified with the help of cause and effect diagram. The experiment comprises of quantitative metrics to analyze the data quality. The research shows that analysis of errors is helpful both for novice and domain experts. However, there is a lack of research that suggests an improvement over identified quality problems. Authors in [14] have validated RDF dataset using constraints that give detailed root cause explanations for all the errors present in the given RDF triple. The framework is validated against SHACL[5] and covers most of the constraints SHACL can validate.

---

[5] https://www.w3.org/TR/shacl/.

3   Recommendations and Future Work

The findings from this survey are (i) lack of end-to-end systems that assess and refine data quality of knowledge graphs, (ii) lack of evaluation methods. The end-to-end system requires a complete understanding of data quality metrics assessment, root causes of violations, and suggestions to refine the triples that do not obey the data quality. The proposed data quality refinement lifecycle, as shown in Fig. 2 includes the following:

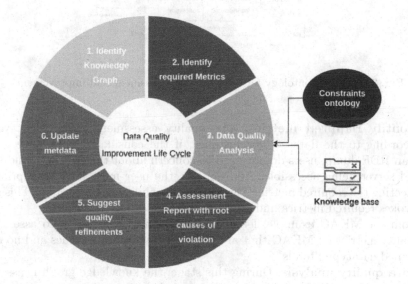

Fig. 2. Stages of ontology based data quality improvement

A ontology Data Quality Assessment and Improvement (DQAI) is proposed and has to be modeled by considering all the stages of lifecycle shown in Fig. 2. Figure 3 describes initial version of the proposed ontology which describes the dataset along with data quality assessment, root causes of violations and improvement classes. Each dataset is assessed using multiple metrics (M1 ...) that belongs to accessible, intrinsic, contextual and representational dimension. Metric is associated with quality violation which describes type of violation associated with the triple. Each type of quality violation is associated with improvement technique.

1. **Identify the Knowledge graph.** The first step is to select a knowledge graph, whose quality has to be analysed. Knowledge graphs follow some structure to store data which is referred as domain ontology. In case of absence of domain ontology, it can be learned from the knowledge graph. DQI stores the knowledge graph under graph class.

   For example, consider Microsoft Academic Knowledge Graph (MKAG) [19]. MKAG ontology has eight classes that are Paper, Affiliation, Field of study etc.

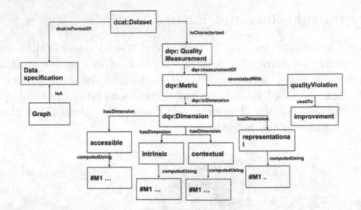

Fig. 3. Proposed ontology for data quality assessment and improvement

2. **Identify required metrics.** The quality assessment requirement varies according to the dataset. For instance, if the considered knowledge graph is an RDF dump, users do not need to concern about the SPARQL endpoint and server being accessible. Additionally, the user must have the option of selecting the required metric. This enables flexibility of the system. This step invokes required metrics under each dimension in DQAI ontology.
From the MKAG example, let us consider a user who wants to assess two quality metrics on MKAG that are syntactically accurate values and no malformed datatype literals.

3. **Data quality analysis.** During this stage, the knowledge graph is assessed against the quality metrics identified and defined in the previous lifecycle stage. The metric implementation can be assisted with domain ontology and a knowledge base. Domain ontology and a knowledge base helps evaluate multiple metrics of intrinsic dimension. These act as rules to evaluate data quality. With the help of reasoning engine, all quality violated triples are stated and stored for further analysis by mapping them to axioms in the data quality ontology. Metrics that are of interest are computed and stored in the ontoloty DQAI.
From the MKAG example, domain ontology of MKAG can be considered. A reasoner based on description logic will infer problematic triples that does not obey the rules mentioned in the knowledge base and ontology. Consider a class 'author' that has properties orcidId and paperCount. PaperCount has a datatype integer that means any value other than integer for this attribute is quality violation as per the definition of the metric 'no malformed datatype'. 'Syntactically accurate values' is computed either with the help of clustering/syntactic rules. Clustering on orcidId would cluster similar id into one/- multiple clusters leaving out the wrongly mapped orcidId. Similarly all other metrics that are of interest to the user are computed on all the properties in the knowledge graph and quality values are computed based on the definitions given to each metric in [51].

4. **Assessment report with root causes of violations.** Data quality assessment report describes the data quality of the knowledge graph for all the metrics chosen in step 2. This report can make use of the data quality vocabulary(DQV) approved by W3 consortium to report data quality assessment score. It will also elucidate triples violating quality constraints along with the precise reason for the violation. While evaluating the data quality metric, it is possible to identify triples that violate the quality metric. These violations are stored in the ontology for subsequent analysis.

5. **Suggest quality refinements/improvements.** Resolving the violations requires refinement process by the framework. Improvement of data quality requires to add/modify/remove the triple violating quality constraint. These automatic suggestions help the user to make a decision. Improvement techniques can be applied on quality violated triples that are stored in DQAI ontology.
   From the MKAG example, for quality violated triples a suggestion should be given to the user. It helps the user to take a decision that helps to improve the quality of the available data.

6. **Update metadata.** In this stage, the knowledge graph is appended with a quality assessment report along with all triples violating quality constraints and suggestions. It helps the user to understand their knowledge graph quality and root causes of triples violating quality constraints before using knowledge graph.
   MAKG example of sample input and expected output for step 4 is as shown in Listing 1.1. Assume that there is wrongly mapped datatype for paperCount, syntactically invalid value for orcidId. Quality violated triples are identified with the help of knowledge base that validates the triples with the given ontology and facts stated by domain experts. The output must identify all triples that do not obey the constraints mentioned in the knowledge base. Expected output shows ill-typed literal and the data quality associated dataset. The further step involves refinement that can make suggestions to add/modify/remove a particular triple.

Listing 1.1. Expected input and output of the proposed method

```
Input:
mk: https://mkag.org/class.
mag: https://makg.org/property.
foaf: http://xmlns.com/foaf/0.1/.
dbo: http://dbpedia.org/ontology.
: http://dataqualityviolation.com/violations.

mk:author dbo:orcidId "1234-2345-1234-43";
          mag:paperCount 12.3;

Expected output:
:violation :type :datatypemismatch ;
           :triple mk:author ;
```

```
             : value  mag : paperCount  ;
             : datatype  xsd : decimal  ;
             : expectedDT  xsd : integer  .

: myDataset  a  dcat : Dataset  ;
             dcterms : title  MAKG  ;
             dqv : hasQualityMeasurement  : somemeasurement  .

: somemeasurement  a  dqv : QualityMeasurement  ;
             dqv : computedOn  : myDataset  ;
             dqv : isMeasurementOf  : inverseFuncmismatch  ;
             dqv : value  ''12''^^xsd : int .
```

Most of the literature have evaluated their model by considering various knowledge graphs rather than comparing their model with similar other models. One of the most significant issues is a diverse format of the quality assessment report because of which it is highly challenging to compare quality assessment results of the models. W3 has defined the data quality vocabulary to describe the results of data quality assessment. Researchers can make use of this vocabulary while publishing data quality assessment results. Another problem is the number of metrics used to assess the model. A solution for such problem requires benchmarking standard collection of metrics as well as an evaluation method with the help of domain experts.

An assessment framework that works on any knowledge graph is a requirement. However, to the best of our knowledge the knowledge graph used for most of the existing research is DBpedia. Researchers have tried to solve quality issues related to DBpedia rather than giving a generic approach. One can use their proposed model on multiple RDF dumps to understand whether the model can identify problems associated with RDF data.

4   Conclusion

This paper presents a survey on knowledge graph assessment and improvement approaches. It can be seen that a larger body of work exists on data quality assessment techniques ranging from an assessment based on a single metric to multiple metrics with different goals. The survey has revealed that there are, at the moment, rarely any approaches which simultaneously assess and refine the knowledge graphs. Most of the literature considers scalability performance as an evaluation method rather than defining the model's accuracy by considering test dataset.

This survey's future work involves modeling an ontology to capture all the data quality violations. It also includes building a knowledge base that can logically reason out violations to locate the quality violated triples. This helps data publishers and consumers understand their data quality along with quality violated triples, if any. A gold standard dataset has to be prepared to all possible violations which can be used to for evaluation purposes.

Acknowledgements. This work was funded by Science Foundation Ireland through the SFI Centre for Research Training in Machine Learning (18/CRT/6183).

References

1. Acosta, M., Zaveri, A., Simperl, E., Kontokostas, D., Flöck, F., Lehmann, J.: Detecting linked data quality issues via crowdsourcing: a DBpedia study, vol. 9, pp. 303–335. IOS Press (2018)
2. Assaf, A., Troncy, R., Senart, A.: Roomba: an extensible framework to validate and build dataset profiles. In: Gandon, F., Guéret, C., Villata, S., Breslin, J., Faron-Zucker, C., Zimmermann, A. (eds.) ESWC 2015 (LNAI and LNB). LNCS, vol. 9341, pp. 325–339. Springer, Cham (2015). https://doi.org/10.1007/978-3-319-25639-9_46
3. Albertoni, R., et al.: Data quality vocabulary (DQV). W3C interest group note. World Wide Web Consortium (W3C) (2015)
4. Almeida, R., Maio, P., Oliveira, P., Barroso, J.: Ontology based rewriting data cleaning operations, vol. 20–22-July-2016, pp. 85–88. Association for Computing Machinery (2016)
5. Arruda, N., et al.: A fuzzy approach for data quality assessment of linked datasets, vol. 1, pp. 387–394. SciTePress (2019)
6. Ballou, D.P., Tayi, G.K.: Enhancing data quality in data warehouse environments. Commun. ACM **42**(1), 73–78 (1999)
7. Behkamal, B., Kahani, M., Bagheri, E.: Quality metrics for linked open data. In: Chen, Q., Hameurlain, A., Toumani, F., Wagner, R., Decker, H. (eds.) DEXA 2015. LNCS (LNAI and LNB), vol. 9261, pp. 144–152. Springer, Cham (2015). https://doi.org/10.1007/978-3-319-22849-5_11
8. Bonatti, P.A., Decker, S., Polleres, A., Presutti, V.: Knowledge graphs: new directions for knowledge representation on the semantic web (Dagstuhl seminar 18371). Dagstuhl Rep. **8**(9), 29–111 (2019)
9. Bozic, B., Brennan, R., Feeney, K., Mendel-Gleason, G.: Describing reasoning results with RVO, the reasoning violations ontology. In: MEPDaW/LDQ@ ESWC. pp. 62–69 (2016)
10. Caminhas, D., Cones, D., Hervieux, N., Barbosa, D.: Detecting and correcting typing errors in DBpedia, vol. 2512. CEUR-WS (2019)
11. Chen, J., Chen, X., Horrocks, I., Jiménez-Ruiz, E., Myklebust, E.B.: Correcting knowledge base assertions. ArXiv abs/2001.06917 (2020)
12. Chen, X., Jia, S., Xiang, Y.: A review: knowledge reasoning over knowledge graph. Expert Syst. Appl. **141**, 112948 (2020)
13. Csáki, C.: Towards open data quality improvements based on root cause analysis of quality issues. In: Parycek, P., et al. (eds.) EGOV 2018. LNCS (LNAI and LNB), vol. 11020, pp. 208–220. Springer, Cham (2018). https://doi.org/10.1007/978-3-319-98690-6_18
14. De Meester, B., Heyvaert, P., Arndt, D., Dimou, A., Verborgh, R.: RDF graph validation using rule-based reasoning. Semant. Web J. **12**(1), 117–142 (2020)
15. Debattista, J., Lange, C., Auer, S.: daQ: an ontology for dataset quality information. In: Central Europe Workshop Proceedings, vol. 1184. CEUR-WS (2014)
16. Debattista, J., Auer, S., Lange, C.: Luzzu-a methodology and framework for linked data quality assessment. J. Data Inf. Qual. **8**(1), 1–32 (2016)

17. Debattista, J., Lange, C., Auer, S.: A preliminary investigation towards improving linked data quality using distance-based outlier detection. In: Li, Y.-F., et al. (eds.) JIST 2016. LNCS, vol. 10055, pp. 116–124. Springer, Cham (2016). https://doi. org/10.1007/978-3-319-50112_39

18. Dimou, A., et al.: Assessing and refining mappings to RDF to improve dataset quality. In: Arenas, M., et al. (eds.) ISWC 2015. LNCS (LNAI and LNB), vol. 9367, pp. 133–149. Springer, Cham (2015). https://doi.org/10.1007/978-3-319-25010-6_8

19. Färber, M.: The Microsoft academic knowledge graph: a linked data source with 8 billion triples of scholarly data. In: Ghidini, C., et al. (eds.) ISWC 2019. LNCS, vol. 11779, pp. 113–129. Springer, Cham (2019). https://doi.org/10.1007/978-3-030-30796-7_8

20. Fürber, C., Hepp, M.: Towards a vocabulary for data quality management in semantic web architectures. In: Proceedings of the 1st International Workshop on Linked Web Data Management, LWDM 2011, pp. 1–8. Association for Computing Machinery, New York (2011)

21. Färber, M., Bartscherer, F., Menne, C., Rettinger, A.: Linked data quality of DBpedia, Freebase, OpenCyc, Wikidata, and YAGO. Semanti. Web 9(1), 77–129 (2018)

22. Hadhiatma, A.: Improving data quality in the linked open data: a survey, vol. 978, p. 012026. Institute of Physics Publishing (2018)

23. Heitmann, B., Hayes, C.: Using linked data to build open, collaborative recommender systems. In: AAAI Spring Symposium: Linked Data Meets Artificial Intelligence, vol. SS-10-07, pp. 76–81 (2010)

24. Kontokostas, D., Westphal, P., Auer, S., Hellmann, S., Lehmann, J., Cornelissen, R.: Databugger: a test-driven framework for debugging the web of data, pp. 115–118. Association for Computing Machinery, Inc. (2014)

25. Kontokostas, D., Zaveri, A., Auer, S., Lehmann, J.: TripleCheckMate: a tool for crowdsourcing the quality assessment of linked data. In: Klinov, P., Mouromtsev, D. (eds.) KESW 2013. CCIS, vol. 394, pp. 265–272. Springer, Heidelberg (2013). https://doi.org/10.1007/978-3-642-41360-5_22

26. Lakshen, G., Janev, V., Vraneš, S.: Challenges in quality assessment of Arabic DBpedia. Association for Computing Machinery (2018)

27. Langer, A., Siegert, V., Göpfert, C., Gaedke, M.: SemQuire - assessing the data quality of linked open data sources based on DQV. In: Pautasso, C., Sánchez-Figueroa, F., Systä, K., Murillo Rodríguez, J.M. (eds.) ICWE 2018. LNCS (LNAI and LNB), vol. 11153, pp. 163–175. Springer, Cham (2018). https://doi.org/10.1007/978-3-030-03056-8_14

28. Lertvittayakumjorn, P., Kertkeidkachorn, N., Ichise, R.: Resolving range violations in DBpedia. In: Wang, Z., et al. (eds.) JIST 2017. LNCS (LNAI and LNB), pp. 121–137. Springer, Heidelberg (2017). https://doi.org/10.1007/978-3-319-70682-5_8

29. Liu, S., d'Aquin, M., Motta, E.: Measuring accuracy of triples in knowledge graphs. In: Gracia, J., Bond, F., McCrae, J.P., Buitelaar, P., Chiarcos, C., Hellmann, S. (eds.) LDK 2017. LNCS (LNAI and LNB), vol. 10318, pp. 343–357. Springer, Cham (2017). https://doi.org/10.1007/978-3-319-59888-8_29

30. Melo, A., Paulheim, H.: Automatic detection of relation assertion errors and induction of relation constraints. Sprachwissenschaft, pp. 1–30 (2020)

31. Mendes, P., Mühleisen, H., Bizer, C.: Sieve: linked data quality assessment and fusion. In: ACM International Conference Proceeding Series, pp. 116–123 (2012)

32. Mihindukulasooriya, N., García-Castro, R., Gómez-Pérez, A.: LD sniffer: a quality assessment tool for measuring the accessibility of linked data. In: Ciancarini, P., et al. (eds.) EKAW 2016. LNCS (LNAI and LNB), vol. 10180, pp. 149–152. Springer, Cham (2017). https://doi.org/10.1007/978-3-319-58694-6_20

33. Mihindukulasooriya, N., Poveda-Villalón, M., García-Castro, R., Gómez-Pérez, A.: Loupe-an online tool for inspecting datasets in the linked data cloud, vol. 1486. CEUR-WS (2015)

34. Mihindukulasooriya, N., Rico, M., García-Castro, R., Gómez-Pérez, A.: An analysis of the quality issues of the properties available in the Spanish DBpedia. In: Puerta, J.M., et al. (eds.) CAEPIA 2015. LNCS (LNAI and LNB), vol. 9422, pp. 198–209. Springer, Cham (2015). https://doi.org/10.1007/978-3-319-24598-0_18

35. Mocnik, F.B., Mobasheri, A., Griesbaum, L., Eckle, M., Jacobs, C., Klonner, C.: A grounding-based ontology of data quality measures. J. Spat. Inf. Sci. **2018**(16), 1–25 (2018)

36. Palmonari, M., Rula, A., Porrini, R., Maurino, A., Spahiu, B., Ferme, V.: ABSTAT: linked data summaries with ABstraction and STATistics. In: Gandon, F., Guéret, C., Villata, S., Breslin, J., Faron-Zucker, C., Zimmermann, A. (eds.) ESWC 2015. LNCS, vol. 9341, pp. 128–132. Springer, Cham (2015). https://doi.org/10.1007/978-3-319-25639-9_25

37. Paulheim, H.: Knowledge graph refinement: a survey of approaches and evaluation methods. Semant. Web **8**(3), 489–508 (2017)

38. Paulheim, H., Bizer, C.: Improving the quality of linked data using statistical distributions, vol. 3. IGI Global (2018)

39. Rahm, E., Do, H.H.: Data cleaning: problems and current approaches. IEEE Data Eng. Bull. **23**(4), 3–13 (2000)

40. Rashid, M., Rizzo, G., Mihindukulasooriya, N., Torchiano, M., Corcho, O.: KBQ - a tool for knowledge base quality assessment using evolution analysis, vol. 2065, pp. 58–63. CEUR-WS (2017)

41. Rico, M., Mihindukulasooriya, N., Kontokostas, D., Paulheim, H., Hellmann, S., Gómez-Pérez, A.: Predicting incorrect mappings: A data-driven approach applied to dbpedia. In: Proceedings of the 33rd annual ACM symposium on applied computing, pp. 323–330. Association for Computing Machinery (2018)

42. Sejdiu, G., Rula, A., Lehmann, J., Jabeen, H.: A scalable framework for quality assessment of RDF datasets. In: Ghidini, C., et al. (eds.) ISWC 2019. LNCS (LNAI and LNB), vol. 11779, pp. 261–276. Springer, Cham (2019). https://doi.org/10.1007/978-3-030-30796-7_17

43. Spahiu, B., Maurino, A., Palmonari, M.: Towards improving the quality of knowledge graphs with data-driven ontology patterns and SHACL. In: Conference of 9th Workshop on Ontology Design and Patterns, pp. 103–117. CEUR-WS (2018)

44. Strong, D.M., Lee, Y.W., Wang, R.Y.: Data quality in context. Commun. ACM **40**(5), 103–110 (1997)

45. Trouillon, T., Dance, C., Gaussier, E., Welbl, J., Riedel, S., Bouchard, G.: Knowledge graph completion via complex tensor factorization. J. Mach. Learn. Res. **18**, 4735–4772 (2017)

46. Vaidyambath, R., Debattista, J., Srivatsa, N., Brennan, R.: An intelligent linked data quality dashboard. In: AICS 27th AIAI Irish Conference on Artificial Intelligence and Cognitive Science, pp. 1–12 (2019)

47. Weiskopf, N., Weng, C.: Methods and dimensions of electronic health record data quality assessment: enabling reuse for clinical research. J. Am. Med. Inform. Assoc. **20**(1), 144–151 (2013)

48. Wienand, D., Paulheim, H.: Detecting incorrect numerical data in DBpedia. In: Presutti, V., d'Amato, C., Gandon, F., d'Aquin, M., Staab, S., Tordai, A. (eds.) ESWC 2014. LNCS (LNAI and LNB), vol. 8465, pp. 504–518. Springer, Cham (2014). https://doi.org/10.1007/978-3-319-07443-6_34

49. Yoo, S., Jeong, O.: Automating the expansion of a knowledge graph. Expert Syst. Appl. **141**, 112965 (2020)

50. Zaveri, A., et al.: User-driven quality evaluation of DBpedia. In: Proceedings of the 9th International Conference on Semantic Systems, pp. 97–104 (2013)

51. Zaveri, A., Rula, A., Maurino, A., Pietrobon, R., Lehmann, J., Auer, S.: Quality assessment for linked data: a survey. Semant. Web **7**(1), 63–93 (2016)

Industrial Control Honeypot Based on Power Plant Control System

Xu Yao[1], Gang Wang[1,2]([✉]), Pei-zhi Yan[2], Li-fang Zhang[1], and Ye Sun[1]

[1] Inner Mongolia University of Technology, Hohhot 010050, China
20191800086@imut.edu.cn
[2] Information Construction and Management Center, Hohhot, China

Abstract. Industrial honeypot is different from ordinary honeypot mainly because of the industrial control protocol used in the communication of industrial control equipment in the industrial control system. The trapping ability of industrial control honeypot mainly depends on its simulation interaction level, and the simulation protocol communication interaction determines the authenticity of the trapping environment. Based on the investigation of the control system of real power plant, it is proposed that the control system of power plant is placed in sandbox to restore the high fidelity of honeypot. Using protocol reverse analysis technology, in-depth analysis of EGD industrial control protocol to master protocol characteristics, timely sense abnormal industrial control traffic data and abnormal protocol packets. Use the Cuckoo sandbox framework to deploy honeypots with the main aircraft deployment mechanism to prevent escape or other sabotage if an attacker identifies the honeypot as a springboard. Finally, all suspected attack data captured by honeypot will be submitted to cuckoo host for analysis, providing reliable data for network security administrators and a more secure active defense network environment for power plants.

Keywords: Honeypot · Industrial control system safety protection · Cuckoo · Abnormal process identification · Protocol Reverse parsing

1 Introduction

With the continuous development of Internet, Internet of Things, 5G and other network technologies, the industrial control system (ICS) [1] network has gradually been connected to the general Internet from a relatively independent and closed network environment. Conforming to the response of the times, the combination of current industrial control systems with a variety of new information technologies has become a development trend in recent years. At the same time, it also brings new tasks and challenges to the network security protection of industrial control systems.

As an important part of the field of industrial control, the power system security is not only a key national infrastructure, but also related to the national economy and people's livelihood, and its network security issues should not be underestimated [2]. As a large number of power industrial control equipment, industrial control protocols, etc.

© Springer Nature Switzerland AG 2022
C. Xu et al. (Eds.): ICWS 2021, LNCS 12994, pp. 77–89, 2022.
https://doi.org/10.1007/978-3-030-96140-4_6

are gradually accessing and approaching the general Internet, the information security threats of the general Internet have gradually penetrated into the traditional power system [3]. Since the industrial control network environment was dominated by physical protection in the early years, the industrial control protocols designed and developed did not consider general Internet threats, and many industrial control pro-tocols lacked security mechanisms. In the smart grid environment, power plant sys-tems will no longer be completely physically isolated, and a lot of data will flow to the corporate intranet or even be completely exposed to the Internet. Since the Stuxnet virus (Stuxnet) incident was exposed in Iran in 2010 [4], various industrial control network security incidents have been frequently exposed abroad [5]. At the end of 2015, the Ukrainian power system was attacked by malware and caused a large-scale blackout [6]. Two large-scale black-outs occurred in Venezuela in 2019 [7]. In May 2021, a large U.S. oil product pipeline transportation company was attacked by ransomware and shut down four of its main oil product pipelines [8]. There is evi-dence that using sound waves, electromagnetic waves, electromagnetic radiation, etc., even an ordinary smart phone can successfully invade a physically isolated computer [9].

Once the power production environment is destroyed or loses control, it will not only have a negative impact on the economy and public safety, but also involve the national security level [10]. In view of the current threats to the power system, honeypot technology is used for active defense, and the power system is protected from threats by traps [11].

Based on the above, this paper designs and implements an industrial control honeypot based on the power plant control system. The main tasks are as follows:

(a) Using the idea of honeypot, combined with sandbox technology, realize a power plant honeypot based on sandbox technology. After on-site inspections of power plants in Inner Mongolia, we have a thorough understanding of the DCS net-work topology and increased the sweetness of honeypots through simulation methods.
(b) This system sets up the client and analysis machine in accordance with cuckoo, and will adopt the capture function of deploying sandbox technology on the client and upload the captured malicious files, malicious traffic and other information to the analysis machine, and use cuckoo's analysis mechanism for analysis.
(c) Through reverse protocol analysis technology, it mainly reversely analyzes the industrial control protocol used in the DCS system of the power plant, improves the EGD private protocol simulation of the industrial control honeypot, deeply analyzes the internal data of the protocol, and analyzes the content of the protocol package of the normal data in the power plant And learn. Capture industrial control data flow, and determine whether there is an abnormality through normal flow distribution.

This system monitors the control system of the power plant by capturing data and the protocol communication of the DCS system of the power plant to realize a honeypot system. The honeypot system will determine the attack data by comparing the captured data with the actual operation level data of the power plant and the actual flow distribu-tion, and identify the attack data through abnormal flow distribu-tion, abnormal process detection, abnormal file access, etc., and protect the power plant from active defense. Control system network.

2 Design of Honeypot Architecture for Power Plant Control System

Since the main determinant of the trapping ability of industrial control honeypots is the simulation ability of honeypots, in view of the existing industrial control honeypots, the high cost of high-interaction honeypots, and the insufficient trapping ability of low-interaction honeypots, this paper proposes to introduce the introduction based on the simulation of power plant control system Sandbox technology puts the power plant control system in the sandbox and runs it as a honeypot. It completes the high simulation of the honeypot while preventing the attacker from identifying the honey-pot and attacking the real device.

The overall architecture of the high-interaction industrial control honeypot designed in this paper is divided into a data analysis module, a data capture module, and a data control module (see Fig. 1). Honeypot simulation module, honeypot analysis module, alarm response module.

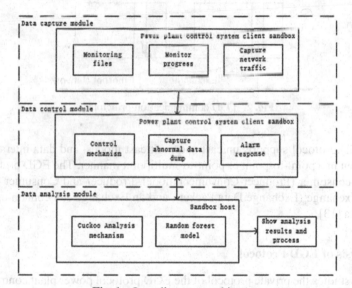

Fig. 1. Overall system architecture

This system uses the cuckoo sandbox analysis mechanism. In order to improve the trapping ability of the industrial control honeypot, the data capture module uses the real power plant control system in the sandbox to form a highly realistic interactive scene. The internal information of the sandbox is monitored and abnormal data is captured. It mainly monitors normal processes, file paths, network traffic, etc., and captures abnormal data that may be caused by attacks to meet the capture requirements of industrial control honeypots. For network traffic monitoring, in addition to the normal communication protocol, it mainly analyzes the private communication protocol EGD protocol adopted by the power generation equipment, and develops and realizes the normal description of the EGD protocol on the basis of this, and identifies non-protocol protocols.

3 Key Technology

EGD agreement, namely Ethernet Global Data Ethernet global data. The EGD proto-col is a universal language applied to electronic controllers [12].

3.1 EGD Protocol Communication

The EGD protocol is an application layer protocol like most industrial control proto-cols. EGD data is periodically sent from one PLC to another (group) PLC. In the EGD communication mode, the communication nodes are divided into Producer and Consumer. The EGD protocol is a UDP/IP-based protocol and occupies UDP port 18246. The principle of EGD communication is shown (see Fig. 2).

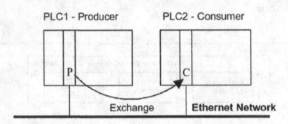

Fig. 2. EGD communication principle

The EGD protocol supports unicast and multicast modes, and data interaction can be carried out in a point-to-point or point-to-multipoint manner. The EGD protocol uses a producer-consumer (Producer-Consumer) model. Producer and Consumer exchange data with Exchange (Exchange Data Packet), and an Exchange can contain up to 1400 bytes of data [13].

3.2 Analysis of EGD Protocol

This article studies the private protocol of the EGD protocol power plant control system communication, as shown in Fig. 3. The EGD protocol is an application layer protocol data packet based on UDP. After the original data is packaged by the EGD protocol, the general data protocol is used to perform the protocol data unit (PDU) Encapsulation, connection and transmission after UDP/IP encapsulation, due to the connectionless and maximum delivery of UDP, and the simple structure of the EGD protocol, the use of EGD protocol communication in the power plant control system communication will also rely on software configuration to a certain extent (see Fig. 3).

IP header	UDP header	EGD header	data

Fig. 3. Format of EGD protocol header

EGD data messages will be sent from the producer to the consumer as required. Each EGD message is mainly divided into two parts: a fixed header and a data message. The header has a fixed format and is composed of 32 bytes. See below for specific protocol analysis (see Fig. 4) (Table 1).

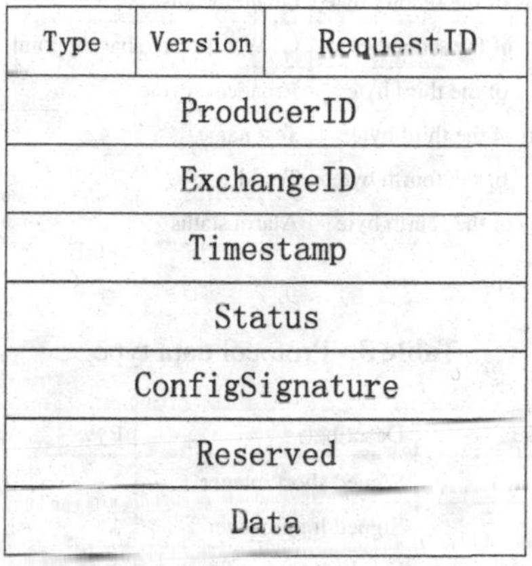

Type	Version	RequestID
ProducerID		
ExchangeID		
Timestamp		
Status		
ConfigSignature		
Reserved		
Data		

Fig. 4. Format of EGD protocol

Table 1. EGD protocol analysis

Field name	Byte	Function and meaning
Type	1	Type, the fixed value is 13
Version	1	Version number, fixed value is 1
Request ID	2	A total of 16 bits are sent according to the number of data packets of each Exchanged ID
Producer ID	4	Sender's IP address
Timestamp	8	Timestamp
Status	4	State default value is 1
Config sigature	4	Configuration signature
Reserved	4	Reserved field, set to 0
Data	Up to 1400	Data content

Combining power plant control system and reverse protocol analysis technology, using packet capture tools and adjusting parameters, using a single variable to analyze and compare the similarities and differences of data packets during different operations. Since the EGD protocol uses the Ethernet structure protocol, network protocol analysis tools such as the packet capture tool Wireshark are used. Detect input digital quantity, output digital quantity, input analog quantity, output analog quantity, etc.

After analysis, the system protocol structure is divided into two fields, value and quality, in the EGD data message part. The quality content has a total of 4 bytes, and the data length is determined by the character type field in the quality content (Table 2).

Table 2. EGD data field analysis

Quality field name	describe
High 4 bits of the first byte	Fixed value 1
Low 4 bits of the first byte	Type of data
High 4 bits of the second byte	Quality status
Low 4 bits of the second byte	GTW software sharing point settings
High 4 bits of the third byte	Broadcast cycle
Low 4 bits of the third byte	Test name
High 4 bits of the fourth byte	Test describe
Low 4 bits of the fourth byte	Alarm status

Table 3. Protocol data type

Type of data	Describe	Byte	Value
INT	Signed short integer	2	0
DINT	Signed long integer	4	1
REAL, float	Single precision floating point	4	2
LREAL, double	Double-precision floating-point number	8	3
UINT	Unsigned short integer	2	4
UDINT	Unsigned long integer	4	5
DWORD	Unsigned long integer	4	6

The data types and specific values used by the communication protocol are shown in Table 3.

3.3 Analysis of EGD Protocol

Cuckoo is an open source automated malware analysis system [14]. It is used to automatically run and analyze files, collect comprehensive analysis results, and outline the behavior of malware when running in an isolated operating system [14]. The whole cuckoo is divided into two parts: Cuckoo Host: Cuckoo's core server, responsible for the initiation of analysis tasks and the generation of analysis results reports, as well as the management of multiple virtual machines. Analysis Guest: The analysis client, where the honeypot will be used as the client for analysis, is responsible for providing a virtual environment for the target sample to run, detecting the running status of the target, and reporting the detected data to Cuckoo Host.

The overall architecture of Cuckoo, the host mainly receives analysis tasks, starts the honeypot as the analysis machine, and transmits the samples and some necessary analysis codes to the client through the http protocol. Cuckoo obtains the behavior of the sample through its internal analysis code, and then after the analysis is completed, the analysis result is transmitted to the host through tcp, and the client is returned to the state of sample execution.

4 System Implementation

The power plant control system honeypot is based on the open source sandbox architecture cuckoo, and is based on the power plant communication protocol EGD private protocol for development and power plant control system business simulation. The power plant control system is placed in the cuckoo sandbox to form a high-interaction simulation Degree honeypot. The entire honeypot system is developed using the Django framework.

4.1 Data Capture Module

The most basic function of a honeypot is to capture all the information about the entire attack process initiated by the attacker on the industrial control system without the attacker noticing it. This system is written in python3 language to complete the capture of industrial control honeypots. It mainly monitors the access file path, process, and network traffic of the system and captures attack information.

The core library for process data monitoring and file data monitoring calls is psutil. The process and file monitoring of the entire power plant operating environment are performed, and the original process whitelist is optimized through the model trained by machine learning, which solves the problem of the traditional whitelist filtering mechanism being single and requiring frequent maintenance. It mainly monitors the related information created by the process and the operation information of the process on the file.

For network traffic information capture, use the scapy library in python to capture system data packets and save them as pacp files. scapy has implemented a large number of network protocols internally, such as DNS, ARP, IP, TCP, UDP, etc., which can be used to write. Dump the captured traffic information to the database through the third-party library. Use the above method to complete the capture function of the power plant's honeypot system.

4.2 Data Control Module

The honeypot system of the power plant takes certain control measures against the attacker on the process, file, network data packet and its flow in order to identify the attack behavior. The captured process file information is passed through the trained model to determine whether it is an abnormal process, and index the abnormal process to detect and alert the illegal process in time, and the client can use whether to block the process to deal with the abnormal process. Call the cuckoo interface for suspected virus files, submit them to cuckoo for analysis and return the analysis results page (see Fig. 5).

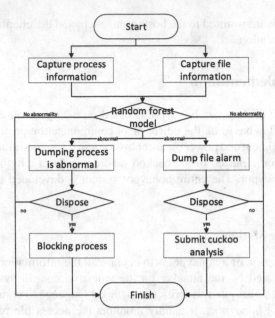

Fig. 5. Process and file monitoring

The application layer recognizes the industrial control protocol message according to the characteristics of the communication protocol message of the power plant, and recognizes its message format (see Fig. 6).

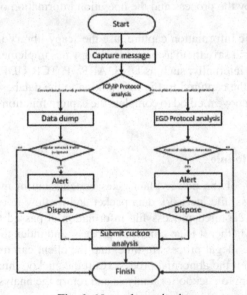

Fig. 6. Network monitoring

4.3 Data Analysis Module

Computer attacks usually cause abnormal operations of processes on files, such as reading, writing, opening, etc. of key files; at the same time, attacks are often accompanied by high CPU utilization and resource usage, as well as memory resource usage, disk space usage, and file operation time. And so on, judge whether it is abnormal data based on information such as the time sequence corresponding to the operation of the trigger file when the process is executed.

(a) Data extraction

Through the process capture tool and the process file module captured by the honeypot, the normal data of the normal process and file data during the operation of the power plant system are extracted. The attack data is mainly downloaded from the website of Eternal Blue virus and Stuxnet virus samples, and the other is to download real attack malware samples from the Honeynet Project website. Run separately and independently in the power plant simulation environment through the process information capture tool to analyze and transfer it to csv format. After the captured data is subjected to feature screening, data dimensionality reduction, and data normalization, the sample situation is shown in Table 4 (Table 5).

Table 4. Sample data overview

Type of data	Number of samples
Normal data	3710
Attack data	2490
Total data	6200

(b) Optimal classification model screening

The captured process data is extracted from the characteristic vector of the process behavior, and the information model of the normal process of the computer is established. Through the operation of the important level of the file by the process, the machine learning training model is used to identify the abnormal process. Since the identification attack problem is a two-class problem, that is, whether it has been attacked. This article mainly uses the following machine learning for modeling training: KNN, logistic regression, random forest, KVM, decision tree. The main evaluation indicators selected are: precision, recall, F1-score, accuracy. See (1)–(4) for detailed evaluation index formulas.

$$Precision = \frac{TP}{TP + FP} \tag{1}$$

$$Recall = \frac{TP}{TP + FN} \tag{2}$$

$$F1\,score = \frac{2TP}{2TP + FP + FN} \tag{3}$$

Table 5. Characteristics of sample data

Serial number	Feature name
1	Process name
2	Associated file name
3	Process execution status
4	Number of open threads
5	Whether to run with privileges
6	Action on the event
7	The name of the user account that performed the operation
8	Resource path referenced by the event
9	CPU utilization
10	Amount of dedicated memory
11	Amount of shared memory
12	File operation time
13	Memory usage
14	Disk space usage
15	Disk response time

$$Acc = \frac{TP + TN}{TP + TN + FP + FN} \tag{4}$$

The evaluation results of the classification algorithm are now shown in the Table 6 below.

Table 6. Comparison of model evaluation results

Model	Precision	Recall	F1score	Acc
KNN	0.948	0.906	0.931	0.931
Logistic regression	0.784	0.889	0.833	0.864
Random forest	1	0.997	0.998	0.999
KVM	0.985	0.914	0.953	0.962
Decision tree	1	0.896	0.945	0.954

The above five classifiers are all trained using the same data set. By comparing the results of the above five classic classification models on the four evaluation indicators, it can be seen that among the five algorithms, the decision tree and random forest classifiers have the highest accuracy. Reached 1, but in other measures such as recall rate, it is not as high as random forest, so random forest classifier is used to analyze the process-related data and determine abnormalities.

For network data, it is divided into two categories: The first category is ordinary network data. The captured abnormal data packets are dumped and alarmed. At the same time, the formed pacp file can be submitted to cuckoo for disposal. The second category is industrial control data packets, which mainly refer to EGD messages. It analyzes the message length of the industrial control protocol and whether the data unit identification information of the industrial control protocol message is complete and correct. According to the analysis result of the message, the message is shunted, and the industrial control protocol message is further analyzed in depth, and the analyzed EGD protocol is used to detect the violation of the protocol on the message.

5 System Testing and Analysis

According to the environmental network structure of the power plant control system, the system backbone network adopts the TCP/IP industrial Ethernet structure design and adopts the standard EGD protocol.

The communication network between the controller and the IO module forms a serial ring network structure through the bus connection of the equipment and the redundant controller, which realizes the real-time data interaction between the IO module and the controller.

Based on the original environment of the power plant, the honeypot of the power plant is now deployed as follows. The honeypot system of the power plant is connected to the real system Ethernet to form a closed loop, and the real system is put into the sandbox through the sandbox client mechanism to simulate one or more real engineering stations or gateway tools. And connect multiple clients with the analysis and management host (see Fig. 7).

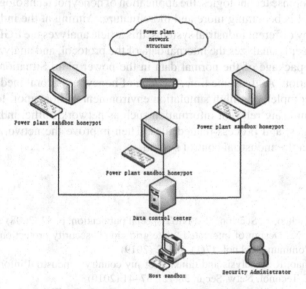

Fig. 7. Environment deployment diagram

System testing is carried out for the industrial control honeypot system of the power plant control system to identify abnormal process data, and give warnings for abnormal data. Display the captured abnormal logs through the background log, and monitor system process abnormalities in real time (see Fig. 8).

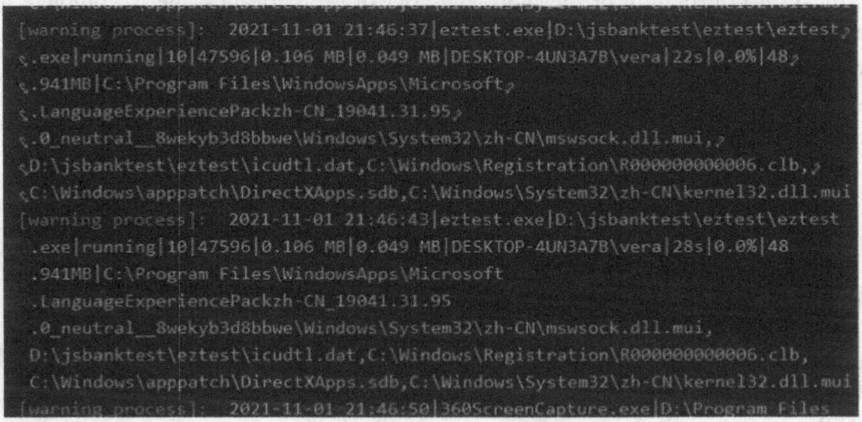

Fig. 8. Identify abnormal process information

6 Conclusion

Among active defense technologies, the application of honeypot technology in the industrial control field is becoming more and more mature. Aiming at the industrial control protocols used by different industrial systems, this article analyzes the EGD communication protocol, deeply analyzes the internal data of the protocol, and analyzes the content of the protocol package of the normal data in the power plant Situation and make an attack identification. At the same time, the idea of honeypot is combined with sandbox technology to complete the high simulation environment of honeypot. Identify abnormalities by monitoring relevant information such as network traffic, industrial control protocol packages, and process-related files. Then improve the network environment security of the entire industrial control system.

References

1. Stouffer, K., Falco, J., Scarfone, K.: NIST special publication, p. 82 (2008)
2. Min, J., Liu, X.: Design of integrated "state grid cloud" security protection system. Electr. Power Inf. Commun. Technol. **17**(1), 78–82 (2019)
3. Dong, L., Zhao, R.: Analysis and thinking of my country's industrial information security situation. Inf. Technol. Netw. Secur. **38**(12), 37–41 (2019)
4. Stevens, C.: Assembling cybersecurity: the politics and materiality of technical malware reports and the case of Stuxnet. Contemp. Secur. Policy **41**(1), 129–152 (2020)
5. Li, D.: Analysis of Stuxnet virus incident and improvement of industrial control security protection capabilities. Netw. Secur. Technol. Appl. (01), 9–10+24 (2019)

6. Mi, X.: From the "Stuxnet virus" and Ukraine power outages to see the information security of electric power companies. Public Power (S2), 50–56 (2016)
7. Zhu, C.: Behind the blackout in Venezuela. State Grid (05), 72–74 (2019)
8. Liu, X.: The "black" of the US oil pipeline may bring ripple effects [ER/OL]. Xinhuanet, http://www.xinhuanet.com/. Accessed 12 May 2021
9. Hu, H.: Physical isolation can also be invaded across networks. China Aerosp. J. (003) (2020)
10. Notice of request for information (RFI) on ensuring the continued security of the united states critical electric infrastructure. The Federal Register/FIND, vol. 86, no. 076 (2021)
11. Zhang, Y., Gao, S., Wang, F., Bian, J.: Overview of industrial control system safety technology research. In: 2018 Proceedings of China Automation Conference (CAC 2018), p. 6. Chinese Society of Automation (2018)
12. GE Energy. GE Fanuc Network and Communication User Manual [ER/OL] (2013). https://www.docin.com/p-1925734744.html
13. Zang, Z.: Research and implementation of industrial gas chromatograph data gateway. China Instr. (06), 36–39 (2020)
14. Cuckoo, [EB/OL]. https://cuckoo.sh/docs/

BCOA: Blockchain Open Architecture

Liang-Jie Zhang[1,2]([✉]), Sheng He[1,3], Jing Zeng[1,2], Yishuang Ning[1,3],
and Huan Chen[1,2]

[1] Kingdee Research, Kingdee International Software Group, Shenzhen 518057, China
[2] National Engineering Research Center for Supporting Software of Enterprise
Internet Services, Shenzhen 518057, China
zhanglj@acm.org
[3] Research Institute of Information Technology, Tsinghua University,
Beijing 100084, China

Abstract. Blockchain as an emerging computing paradigm has revolutionized the next generation internet. The design and realization of blockchain in multiple industries are very challenging tasks due to the complexity of blockchain. Firstly, it refers to the integrations of multiple technologies within communications, distributed system and security. Secondly, it lacks systematic method and theory to guide developers to design the business solutions. To facilitate the down-to-earth application of blockchain, we propose a BlockChain Open Architecture (BCOA) as a reference architecture which divides the blockchain into nine layers: interactions, scenarios, services, components, infrastructure, integration, data architecture, security and privacy and governance. It allows the designers and developers to use this methodology to speedily design solutions for blockchain applications. Finally we use two cases to demonstrate the feasibility and effectiveness of the proposed architecture.

Keywords: Blockchain · Open architecture · Reference architecture

1 Introduction

Blockchain as a popular word has appeared in various IT communities in recent years, however the concept of blockchain refers to multiple technologies including distributed system, P2P communications and security related technologies, etc. These concepts or words are uneasy for common individuals. Besides, no feasible design methodology focuses on how an effective and efficient blockchain based application to be created.

Existing blockchain solutions are diverse and trivial. Especially, designing a blockchain application is a quite challenging task. First, most solutions of blockchain are domain-specific that is quite limited in the extendibility of solutions. Second, the blockchain is the inter-disciplinary integration which is difficult for a designer to get a systematic view for overall solutions. Third, it still lacks a framework currently to tell the blockchain practitioners what a real blockchain application is and how to design a blockchain solution.

To address the above challenges, we propose a blockchain open architecture (BCOA) which allows the designer to gain the methodology to design a blockchain based application. Essentially, it divides the whole architecture [1] into nine core elements. They are interactions, scenarios, services, components, infrastructure, integration, data architecture, security and privacy, and governance. In these elements, interactions includes the interaction manner and interaction mechanism, such as web, mobile client, etc. Scenarios demonstrate the application scenarios about blockchain, they can be applied in various industries. Services are the reusable workflow that is related to blockchain, such as node management service, role management service, etc. Components are the basic elements for enabling blockchain services, they can include smart contract, consensus mechanism, etc. Integration is to address the data bus, communication protocol, platform service, etc. Data architecture is concerned with the block data structure and chain data structure which are corresponding to specific applications. Security and privacy are to address data security and privacy for blockchain. Governance is about the laws, rules, and principles associated with the blockchain, which is determined by the policy and standard of government and organizations. Infrastructure refers to all supporting system that includes computing, storage, and communications.

The reminder of this article is organized as follows: In Sect. 2, we present the blockchain open architecture. Section 3 introduces the case study about BCOA. In Sect. 4, we summarize the conclusions to the article.

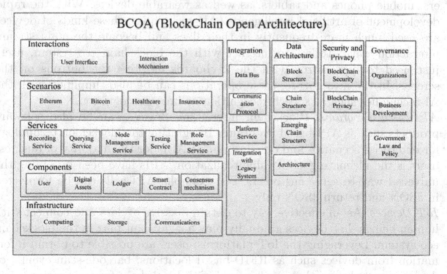

Fig. 1. BlockChain Open Architecture (BCOA)

2   Blockchain Open Architecture

In this section, we present a blockchain open architecture (BCOA), as the Fig. 1 shown, it is divided into nine layers.

2.1   Layer One: Blockchain Interactions

This layer gives the interaction methodology of blockchain. On this layer, the roles of interactions can be human beings, computers, and other devices. In this section, we firstly introduce the user interface of interactions with blockchain, and then describe the interaction mechanism of blockchain.

User Interface: Blockchain is regarded as the next generation of transaction system. Like other application systems, user interface is the direct entry between users and the blockchain eco-system. The main interaction forms can be hardware, software such as web interface or API-based services, embedded systems and even Internet of Things (IoT) devices.

- *Web Interface.* The web interface (also called webUI) provides an easy way to access all settings, configure add-ons as well as graphic views. Through the web interface, users are able to send transactions to the blockchain for processing and see what was happening instead of having to watch a bunch of terminal windows.
- *Interaction Hardware.* Interaction devices include but not limited to computers, mobile phones and tablets, as well as wearable devices. With the rapid development of artificial intelligence (AI) techniques, these kinds of devices are used much more frequently in their lives and become the main stream interaction ways. Today, to interact with the blockchain eco-system, users just need to type words with the keyboards or press the buttons on the screens. In the near future, these operations can be also simplified with the AI techniques such as speech recognition or image recognition.
- *API-based Programs.* Blockchain interaction devices can be also software products such as API-based Programs. Integrating the blockchain technology for enterprise scenarios and opening up the APIs for the majority of business users is the ultimate goal of value realization. APIs have been becoming the universal way to serve customers. For example, API calls can be formatted in JSON and return JSON only.
- *IoT Devices.* As an effective way to obtain massive of data and connect with human beings, IoT devices gradually play a significant part in the blockchain eco-system. Leveraging the IoT platforms, users are possible to obtain information from devices such as RFID-based locations, barcode-scan events, or device-reported data that can be used with blockchain for transactions. IoT Devices will be able to communicate with blockchain-based ledgers to update or validate smart contracts.

Interaction Mechanism: Blockchain technology is a proven, highly secure decentralized digital currency system [3]. In this system, the key point to determine quality of service (QoS) and user experience is to design a harmonious, user-friendly interaction mechanism. As the core component of blockchain, blockchain interaction units (BIUs) are kiosks established in certain places where people can come and operate only with their coin wallets no matter whether it is a mobile or a computer.

These BIUs will connect to the blockchain network just like any other device, thus transactions can be carried out as public service initiatives. Instead of relying on a central authority or trusted intermediary, such as a bank or brokerage firm, to validate transactions, members of a blockchain network use a consensus mechanism as a basis of ensuring trust, accountability, and transparency across the network.

2.2   Layer Two: Scenarios

As a type of distributed ledger that can record transactions between multiple parties efficiently, blockchain is secure by design and is an example of a distributed computing system with high Byzantine fault tolerance. Therefore, it has many promising application scenarios for different fields.

Bitcoin: The first blockchain was conceptualized in 2008 by an anonymous person or group known as Satoshi Nakamoto. It is implemented as a core component of bitcoin to serve as the public ledger for all transactions in 2009 [3]. The invention of the blockchain for bitcoin made it the first digital currency to solve the double-spending problem without the need for a trusted authority or central server. By using a blockchain, bitcoin became the first digital currency to solve the double-spending problem without requiring a trusted administrator and has been the inspiration for many additional applications.

Ethereum: Ethereum is an open source public blockchain platform which was firstly proposed by Vitalik Buterin [4] in 2013. The most important technical contributions of Ethereum are the smart contracts which are programs stored on block keys that can assist and validate the negotiation and operation of contracts. The token issued on the Ethereum blockchain is called Ether that can be traded in many cryptocurrency foreign exchange markets. It is also the media to pay for transaction fees and computing services.

Supply Chain: In the supply chain field, a blockchain system can record the data generated by each party along the supply chain and add it to the transaction record on the shared ledger. It can then be accessed by multiple parties on that shared ledger. For example, planters can see market information about the time/location of purchase and demand and consumer preferences on the shared ledger. This provides planters with more information about consumption and improves their ability to match production with demand. Conversely, supermarkets and consumers can have a greater level of understanding of the product inputs, especially at the farm level, with input data and production location easily verifiable.

As for the manufacturing industry, manufacturers can include who designed a part, its specifications, and the history of each iteration in the blockchain.

Within this same chain, a manufacturer can also record where each instance of a part was made, and what machine made it.

Enterprise Resource Planning (ERP): ERP is an essential part of an enterprise or organization, as it handles finances, invoices, purchase orders and payments. Due to the security benefits and transparent characteristics for all participants, blockchain technology provides rich use cases and can be easy to integrate with the ERP platform. Such integration ensures true data interoperability for various commercial and banking services like online payments, trade financing and contract management facilities, and establishes trust between disparate companies.

Healthcare: Blockchain offers a promising new distributed framework to amplify and to support the integration of health care information. For this application scenario, blockchain can be used in many aspects including the precision medicine initiative, patient care and outcome research (PCOR). The decentralized structure can be used to realize the benefits of improved data integrity and reduce transaction costs.

Insurance: Nowadays, processing payments for insurers still poses challenges in practice. There are not only high processing fees from banks but also at great expense. With the blockchain technology, all the transactions can be stored in a chain of data blocks, thus helping the insurance industry to automate processes such as claim payments.

2.3   Layer Three: Services

The service layer of blockchain includes functional modules that can be configured and reused in different application scenarios. Based on the design architecture of software as a service (SaaS) or function as a service (FaaS), the blockchain service layer can provide "on-demand and ready to use", multi-tenant, scalable and easy to combine technical support for various application scenarios.

Recording Service: The record service should be the unique method that users can write to the blockchain ledger. Record service provides some unified interfaces that support different business scenarios and data formats. Record service provides a standard return data format so that the application layer can realize the status of the record response.

Based on the recording services, the transaction intermediaries can provide transaction services for ordinary users. For different business scenarios, the fundamental service providers will use recording service interfaces to link to the business systems and provide the blockchain services to ordinary users.

Querying Service: The query service should provide a query interface for business related data. The input and output format of the query service depends on the data standards of the specific service. From the query perspective, the blockchain is similar to a database service, but it records the current data as well as the whole history of the data. Benefitting from the query service, the blockchain users can meet the requirement for data verification or verification. Query services must be combined with the role management services to ensure the right or privacy of data on the blockchain.

Node Management Service: Node management service provides the management of the blockchain node, including start-up, joining the blockchain network, and also monitoring the operation status of the nodes. A blockchain browser is usually needed to explore the block and transaction information. Node management services are generally only used by the blockchain node operators. The actual motivation for operating a node should be driven by the internal incentives on the blockchain, or by the external incentives from the real business.

Role Management Service: Role management service provides the management of users and user's permissions, basically including the user's registration, login, logout, and assignment of permissions. In blockchain services, the user's identity should be closely linked to the digital certificate to indicate uniqueness. The role permissions can generally be divided into two categories. One is the blockchain system permissions, including the node administrator (i.e. the blockchain node operator) and the general user (who don't run a blockchain node by himself). Another is the business system permissions which generally determine the role in the actual business, e.g. the seller, buyer, guarantor in an asset auction. The actual role of the business system is defined by the business system developer. However, the developer does not necessarily have administrator privilege on the blockchain, because the developer does not have to operate a real blockchain node.

Testing Service: Testing service is designed to help business developers to test smart contracts to develop the real business system on the blockchain. Testing service will enable smart contracts to be written in a complete and unbiased way to express the designed business intent. Ideally, testing services should provide some common and necessary functional modules to speed up the development of smart contracts.

2.4   Layer Four: Components

User. A user is a person with a digital identity on the blockchain. The user component includes data that a person can have a real identity on the blockchain. In addition to the necessary digital certificates and keys, users can also include some real-world personal information to complete identity verification. In the blockchain world, the user data is like a human being which should be unique. The user has digital assets belonging to him/her and has a permission rule to operate the related things.

Digital Assets. Digital assets are objects which have uniqueness on the blockchain. Digital assets on the blockchain provide a unified storage format, invoke interfaces and access rights for data in the same business system. Digital assets provide an informational basis for digitizing physical assets and expressing the data wealth in the blockchain.

Ledger. The collection of users and digital assets make up the blockchain ledger. The ledger is a distributed database of blockchain system which not only holds all current data but also all historical data. The immutable historical data is the most important feature technically of blockchain. Although the current existing blockchain ledger commonly stored in a chain structure, this data structure may evolve in the future. The ledger as a blockchain database supports the realization of the query service, while smart contracts will define the interface implementation of recording service.

Smart Contract. A smart contract defines the relationship and permissions between the users and the digital assets. It is the programmed implementations of business logic on the blockchain. The smart contract is usually triggered by the service layer operation, then executes some code logic, finally interacts with the ledger and response the result to the request. The smart contract is a programmed and unified language on the blockchain distributed system or saying the smart contract is the law or business rule in the world composed by the users and digital assets.

Consensus Mechanism. Consensus mechanism and inter-node communication ensure the consistency of the ledgers between blockchain nodes. For the public blockchain, the consensus mechanism also determines the incentives for nodes, e.g. the miner in Bitcoin. The consensus mechanism determines the disaster tolerance of the blockchain system and it is also the most important impact on declining system performance compared to the existing centralized system. Hence the final consensus mechanism needs to balance among the intensity of trust and robustness from blockchain and the efficiency of the business system [5].

2.5   Layer Five: Blockchain Infrastructure

Cloud infrastructure is fundamental and pervasive for cloud services, including for blockchain services. Besides, unlike traditional cloud services, blockchain, especially the public chain, can be distributed deployed on personal computers. Each personal computer can play the role of computing node in the public chain. Nodes that participate in the calculation all over the world are parts of the blockchain network. In such a scenario, each computer can be considered as a standalone server.

The data storage system of a consortium blockchain is usually in the form of NoSQL, but one can also apply a relational database instead. Blockchain essentially exists in the form of a distributed database, but different from it, blockchain data cannot tamper. In practice, the blockchain such as the one for Bitcoin applies Berkeley DB, which is a file data database, for its wallet. At the same time, it uses Level DB, which is a Key-Value database, for indexing the UTXO and storage blocks.

Merkle Tree [3] is widely used in the blockchain ecosystem and encryption systems, which is commonly known as a hash tree. The Merkle tree is a tree data structure that particularly suitable for storing hash values. The leaf of a Merkle tree is the hash of a data block. The non-leaf node is hash of the concatenated string of its corresponding child nodes.

In blockchain transactions, the Merkle tree is widely deployed. Each transaction will generate a hash value, and then continue to make different hash value operations. Ultimately it will generate a unique node, named Merkle root. Data block will use such a Merkle root as the block header. The results of applying such a processing scheme and data structure help to ensure every transaction unforgeable.

Layer five includes a very fundamental component named P2P (Peer to Peer) network. The echo node in a P2P network has equivalent weight and provides services together without a central or dominant node. In other words, the P2P network does not include any centralized services and hierarchical structure.

P2P network communication sometimes requires encryption. The encryption algorithms applied in blockchain can be roughly divided into three sub-types, namely symmetric encryption, asymmetric encryption and the hybrid combination of both.

The significant component is a digital signature, also known as a public key digital signature. Digital signatures are mainly used for signer identification of transactions and non-repudiation.

Nowadays, many financial organizations, such as banks, insurance companies and securities companies are trying to solve business problems by using blockchain technology. In the deployment phase, we may consider the following strategies and questions.

- The type of blockchain, private chain, public chain or consortium chain?
- The type of deployment platform, public cloud, private cloud, hybrid cloud or PCs.
- How to isolate the business data to the blockchain as a service (baas) while linking the business logic to the baas?
- How to connect the blockchain to legacy logics and applications? Legacy data is of historical value. Often the data is stored in relatively old or cold devices, for example, those legacy devices. The infrastructure layer should provide a fully accessible IOs for connecting the legacy data.

2.6   Layer Six: Integration

In recent years, the need to break the communication barriers between different blockchains becomes significant. Layer six mainly enables data transmission, data formatting and protocol conversion functionalities. The key component played as a medium is named 'messaging system'. The role of a message system includes asynchronous processing, reducing the operation peak, decoupling, etc.

Message systems are versatile. However, selecting a message system in blockchain needs to carefully consider its persistence, capacity, high availability, scalability, compatibility, maintenance, loss rate and workload [6].

To ensure that the data is transmitting correctly, we involve a two-phase process in the architecture. First, the data is validated or formal examination. In the second step, the data is changed into a new format followed by a final transmission. Based on these steps, the underlying of blockchain can be also abstracted as services via encapsulated APIs in the given blockchain implementation platform.

2.7 Layer Seven: Blockchain Data Architecture

The basic data architecture of blockchain refers to a set of transactions stored in the blocks linked via a hash to form the chain structure. Block and chain are the primary elements for blockchain no matter that it is a public blockchain, a private blockchain or a consortium blockchain. Block can be treated as a unit for saving the transactions record, and each block has a previous block except the genesis block which is the first created block in blockchain. Chain is created among blocks by the hash within the headers of blocks. Therefore, it is tricky to falsify the data in the blocks due that the hash will be completely changed if the transactions are modified in blocks.

Block Structure. Block is a basic structure for stored the transactions or ledgers. Usually, the block can include the following four elements: block size, block header, transaction counter, and transactions. As can be shown in Table 1, block size denotes the size of block, block header records the meta data of current block, Transaction counter represents the number of transactions recorded in blocks, transactions are the payload data in block, they are the variables and can be defined according to the requirements of diverse application scenarios.

Table 1. The structure of block

Field	Description
Block Size	Identity of the block
Block Header	Metadata of current block
Transaction	Payload data in block
Transactions Counter	The number of transactions

For the header of block, public blockchain, consortium blockchain and private blockchain can be flexibly defined. The common parts are a timestamp, previous block hash and current block hash.

In the public blockchain field, well-known examples are Bitcoin and Ethereum. Taking bitcoin as an example, as shown in Table 2, the bitcoin block header consists of version, previous block header hash, Merkle root hash, time, n-Bits and nonce. The block version number specifies which set of block validation rules to follow. Previous block header hash guarantees that no previous block can be modified. Merkle root is derived from hashes of all transactions

Table 2. The header structure of block in bitcoin

Size	Field	Description
4 bytes	Version	The block version number indicating the validation rules to follow
32 bytes	Previous Block Header Hash	A hash linked to previous block
32 bytes	Merkle Root Hash	Derived from hashes of all transactions in this block
4 bytes	Time	A Unix timestamp when starting hash the header by the miner
4 bytes	n-Bits	A threshold that this hash must be less than or equal
4 bytes	Nonce	Nonce is random number in order to produce a hash which less than the threshold

in this block, which can ensure none of the transactions can be altered without modifying the header. Time is a Unix timestamp when starting hash the header by the miner. n-Bits is a threshold that this hash must be less than or equal. A nonce is a random number in order to produce a hash which less than the threshold.

Table 3. The structure of block in hyperledger fabric

Field	Description
Block Number	Identity of the block
Block Hash	Block hash similar with public blockchain
Previous Block Hash	Link the block to a chain
Channel Number	The communication linked peer and orderer
Data Hash	Hash of payload in transactions
Transactions Counter	The number of transactions

Regarding to consortium blockchain, it is more flexible than public blockchain due to the difference of consensus mechanism. The block data structure of consortium blockchain can be adaptively defined by business requirements from real scenarios. Typically, Hyperledger Fabric [15] is a consortium blockchain that has the same data items with public blockchain but much simpler, as shown in Table 2, it is the basic header of a block in consortium blockchain.

Chain Structure. Even if block is the basic data element in blockchain, chain structure is the primary feature for blockchain. The chain aims to protect the transaction from modifying.

Fig. 2. The chain structure of blockchain

To retrospect the transaction record according to specific demands of applications, the hash value is the core part in chain structure, as Fig. 2 demonstrates. Each block is linked to the previous block via a previous hash. Therefore, for all blockchains, they usually have the block hash, timestamp and previous block hash. Hash functions can be chosen according to different requirements, such as SHA-128, SHA-256, MD5, etc. The genesis block is the source of this chain.

Emerging Chain Structure. Some emerging chain structures have appeared with the development of blockchain, IOTA [8] is coined for addressing the transaction in the IoT domain. Directed Acyclic Graph (DAG) is used to replace the traditional blockchain structure. For IOTA, each block can have multiple previous blocks and furthermore they form a directed acyclic graph. By this structure, they advocate that the transactions can free regardless of transaction size, the confirmation can be speedy and the transaction number is unlimited. These advantages are the improvement for public blockchain, however, it may to some extent use a centered mechanism to control the chain increment. In this point, it is not fit for the original intention of blockchain thinking.

The Realization of Data Architecture. The blockchain data architecture is an essential part for enabling blockchain applications. The blockchain concept is relatively open and it imposes major concerns on the trustworthy of ledger storage in a distributed environment.

For improving the data architecture, we should consider three parts: inner block data by custom definition, cross-chain integration protocol, link to the smart contract. Regarding block data definition, the block data can be represented as a string or JSON format, the field of header data can be further designed except block hash and previous block hash. The payload data of block should be devised according to the business needs of applications.

Existing protocols of blockchain are in the same type of chain, cross-chain protocol, we can use an XML based protocol by HTTP to integration and keep collaborating with other types of chains. Extended Business Collaboration (EBC) [9] can be employed as a reference solution for conducting cross-chain data integration and interchange. It focuses on bridging the gap of interaction among the multi-organizations. And it provides a semantic model to describe multi-organization collaboration. The blockchain can be seen as a service, the blockchain for different chains are interacted via a Collaborative Exchange Protocol (CxP) to denote business processes.

The smart contract is used to conduct the operation for data in a blockchain. In public blockchain, smart contract is enabled by a programming language such as solidity [10]. It is compiled to EVM code and is sent to blockchain network by RPC. In the consortium blockchain area, such as Hyperledger Fabric, it uses the Go language code to realize the data operation

2.8   Layer Eight: Security and Privacy

Security and Privacy play a critical role in the blockchain. Trustworthy is the basic characteristic for blockchain which focuses on ensuring the trust mechanism for multi-organization participation. Security and privacy solutions can be used in blockchain based on multiple technologies.

Security. *Data Encryption.* Data security is a key issue because all the transactions in blockchain are required to be protected by encryption technologies. For the security of blockchain, it can ensure the security of the sender of the transaction. The security should consider two parts: data security and data manipulation.

To guarantee the security of data of the transaction, multiple encryption approaches can be considered as the candidate solutions. Usually, the encryption algorithm can be divided into symmetric encryption and asymmetric encryption. The symmetric encryption has the same secret key, therefore it is more computing-efficient, but it must firstly share the secret key result in easily exposing the key, while the asymmetric encryption has a different secret key, which owns much higher security because it is no need to share the key beforehand.

Many symmetric encryption algorithms [11] can be used in the blockchain solution, such as DES, 3DES, AES, IDEA. All these algorithms have diverse encryption strength and security levels. Developers can choose the algorithms according to their business requirements. Asymmetric encryption [12] includes RSA, ElGamal, elliptic curve algorithm, etc.

Another emerging encryption algorithm is holomorphic encryption. It allows us to directly processing the ciphertext, which has the same results with encryption after processing for plaintext. It has the application value in cloud based platform; users can upload their data safely via holomorphic encryption. Currently, few practical technologies are applying homomorphic encryption in a real scenario.

Data manipulation for transaction data greatly affects data integrity. Hash based algorithms are employed to address malicious manipulation on the process of data transmission. Hash is a fingerprint for plaintext, which can map the binary value of plaintext into a fixed binary hash value. Current algorithms [12] can be used for blockchain such as MD5, SHA-224, SHA-256, SHA-512. They have a different length about the hash value.

Digital Signature. User identity is also critical in the data transmission of blockchain. By using the digital signature, it can counter the denial of persons in data transactions. In blockchain scenarios, for example, A sends to B a transaction data, how B knows it is sent by A. Here, A firstly makes a digest for the transaction data via hash and then encrypts it using the private key. A sends the transaction data and encrypted string to B. Subsequently, B deciphers the encrypted data by using public key and compares with the hash to validate whether it sent by A or is modified in the communication.

Typical digital signatures, like HMAC [14], blind signature [13] and multi-signature [13], are widely used in blockchain digital signature. HMAC is a hash-based authentication code, the basic procedure is to encrypt the message by shared symmetrical secret key and hash algorithm to conduct encryption to gain the HMAC value. HMAC suppliers can prove they own shared symmetrical secret key, and the sent message can use HMAC to ensure it not falsified by others. Blind signature is to sign under the condition without watching the original content for the message. Blind signature aims to protect the signature from unlinkability.

Privacy. *User Privilege Management.* User privilege management is the core of blockchain privacy [16]. For public blockchain, user privilege is relatively free, all the users are identified by his digital certification. For example, the Bitcoin is to proceed with transactions based on user's digital signature. The address of the account of Bitcoin is the hash string used to distinctively identify the user account in Bitcoin. In consortium blockchain, user privilege management is stricter than public blockchain due that the chain is comprised of multiple peers built via the organizations trusting for each other. For Hyperledger fabric, user privilege is to join identity and role. They manage the peer of blockchain by PKI. The platform can restrict access of peers and clients.

User Digital Certificate. Users can be anonymization via PKI [17]. PKI is a generic framework based on public and private keys to realize safely and reliable message transmission and identity confirmation. The PKI includes Certification Authority (CA), Registration Authority (RA) and certificate database. CA is responsible for certificate announcement and cancellation, which receives the request from RA. RA is to validate the user identity and to verify the legality of data, and it registers and reviews to send to CA. Certificate database is used to store the certificates of blockchain, it can use LDAP service and X.500 format for storage.

The public blockchain is simpler than consortium blockchain which uses traditional PKI. For consortium blockchain, the certificate can include three types including enrollment, transaction and TLS. Enrollment certificate is issued to peers or users registered evidence, it can be effective for a long time. A transaction certificate is issued to a specific user who may conduct a transaction in the blockchain, which is utilized to control the privilege for the transaction and is valid in a short period. The third certificate is to control the access of the blockchain network and protect it from being eavesdropped.

2.9 Layer Nine: Blockchain Ecosystem Governance and Management

The governance and management of the blockchain ecosystem aim to blockchain related laws, rules, and standards. The blockchain also attracts many countries' attention due to its applications in multiple domains. Different counties can have diverse laws and rules for the governance of blockchain.

For the European (EU), the EU Commission provides visibility to blockchain and builds on existing initiatives, consolidates expertise and addresses the challenges created by the new paradigms enabled by blockchain. Fintech is a policy priority of the European Commission since it can and will play a major role in achieving the objectives related to the development of the single market, banking union, the capital markets union and retail financial services [18].

- The EU Commission works with members stated to focus on investment in public-private partnerships by investing resources for development in digital technologies and digital industrial platforms including cloud infrastructure.
- The commission launched the Digitizing European Industry initiative (DEI) is part of the digital single market strategy, where it aims to reinforce the EU's competitiveness in digital technologies and to ensure that every business in Europe, whichever the sector and wherever the location, it can draw benefit from digital innovation.

DEI consists of 5 pillars:

1. EU platform of a national initiative on digitizing industry
2. Digital innovation for all strengthen leadership through partnerships and industrial platforms
3. Digital framework adapting workforce and our education and learning system together.

For the United State, United State jointing Economic Committee Report officially endorses blockchain technology and cryptocurrencies in the US [19].

- Currently, cryptocurrency is taxed as property under US tax laws, making transactions and appreciations in value subject to income and capital gains taxes. The report acknowledges that the current tax structure could freeze investment and exploration into new virtual currencies, especially for smaller transactions such as coffee purchases.
- Uniform Law Commission creates consistent state laws that approve legislation and define what virtual currency business need to file to become money transmitters.
- Money transmission is unable to allow mass-adoption of cryptocurrency, which is difficult to transfer fiat money into crypto currencies.
- US Congress needs to find solutions that balance the needs of consumer protection, security and entrepreneurship.

Regarding to Singapore, in the wake of an increasing in the number of initial coin offerings (ICOs) in Singapore as a means of raising funds, on August 1, 2017, the Monetary Authority of Singapore (MAS) issued a statement clarifying that the offer or issue of digital tokens in Singapore will be regulated by the MAS, if the digital tokens fall within the definition of "securities" regulated under the security laws [20].

- MAS's position is not to regulate virtual currencies. "However, MAS has observed that the function of digital tokens has evolved beyond just being a virtual currency" the statement said.
- Following the August statement, the Deputy Prime Minister and Minister in Charge of MAS (DPM) responded to questions from the Parliament for its sitting on October 2, 2017, on the regulation of cryptocurrencies and ICOs.
- According to the DPM, although the MAS does not regulate virtual currencies, it regulates activities involving the use of virtual currencies that fall under MAS's regulatory ambit, such as money laundering and terrorism financing. The MAS is working on a new regulatory framework for payments that will address the risks associated with virtual currencies, the DPM said.
- With respect to ICOs, the MAS has not issued specific legislation, but will continue to monitor developments and to consider more targeted legislation when it becomes necessary, the DPM added.
- With respect to the new payment regulatory framework, the MAS issued a consultation paper proposing the Payment Services Bill in November 2017.
- The proposed Bill would expand the scope of regulated payment activities to include virtual currency services and other innovations. Under the new framework, entities carrying out virtual currency services including buying or selling virtual currency would be required to be licensed.

Organizational Issues in a blockchain project commonly need to create a study group or a center of excellence on blockchain. Workshops within organization are organized to propagate the knowledge of blockchain and to explore scenarios with the social teams.

3 Case Study

In this section, we will use a B2B e-commerce market case and an accounting blockchain case to demonstrate the feasibility and effectiveness of our proposed architecture. For designing the blockchain solutions for this application, we use the proposed BCOA to conduct the design process.

3.1 B2B E-Commerce Market

Interactions. A mobile app is devised to the B2B e-commerce order management due to the requirements of mobile sales. To address the interactions, we use a small program in WeChat framework to create a user-friendly UI, the demo UI

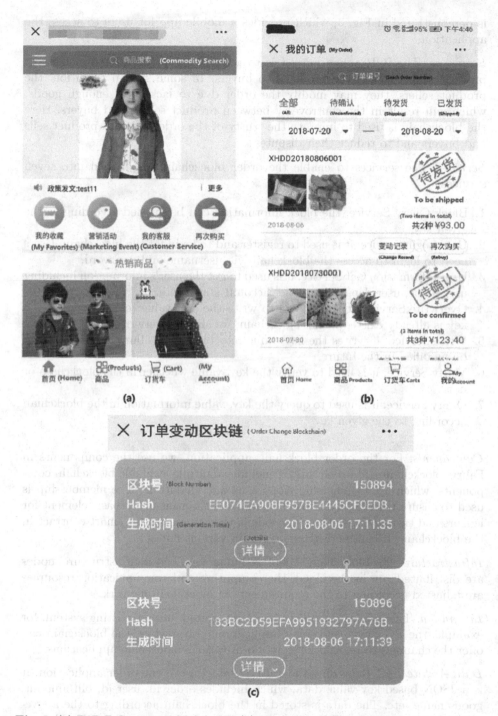

Fig. 3. (a) B2B E-Commerce Mobile UI, (b) The order of B2B online market, (c) The blockchain use in order of B2B online market

is demonstrated in Fig. 3, which provides a mobile app for users to access the application.

Scenarios. The B2B online market is to provide online sales for franchiser or product sellers to sell the products to buyers. In some special condition, the product sellers, they may modify the order due to lacking of enough goods, which will result in the controversy between product sellers and buyers. Here the blockchain is used to improve the trusty of the order between product sells and buyers and to reduce their disputes.

Services. The services to enable the order blockchain are divided into seven services.

1. Block Query Service: the block information can be queried according to the given key.
2. User Login Service: it is used to register and to login for the blockchain. Users need to login to access the blockchain via username and password.
3. User Information Get Service: it is used to get the user's information including user name, user department, user account status, etc.
4. Overwrite Service: it is designed to write the key, value to blockchain if the key is already existed in the blockchain, we should overwrite it.
5. Write Service: it writes the key, value into blockchain, but the value cannot be modified in the future.
6. Verify Service: it is used to verify the key, value whether in the blockchain or not.
7. Query Service: it is used to query the key, value information in the blockchian according to the given key.

Components. For the order blockchain application, we use the components in Fabric blockchain [15] framework, it includes multiple available blockchain components, which are membership, consensus and chaincode. The membership is used to ensure the identity of blockchain, the consensus is the basic element for ledgers and transactions. The chaincode is used to realize the smart contract in the blockchain. It can be distributed run in various nodes.

Infrastructure. The blockchain is deployed in a cloud based infrastructure, nodes are distributed run in the cloud, the computing and communication resources are adjusted according to the requirements of blockchain network.

Integration. The application allows being integrated into an existing system, for example, the PC client, and other applications. Meanwhile, the blockchain can offer the channels to realize the isolation of various blockchain applications.

Data Architecture. Regarding the data architecture to the order application, it is a JSON based key-value data, which includes order id, user id, bill amount, goods name, etc. The data is stored in the blockchain according to the above-mentioned services. It will be conducted via a smart contract or chaincode.

Security and Privacy. The order data will be encrypted by an elliptic curve algorithm and different users are completely isolated according to their access authority. Users can only access their data.

Governance. For the blockchain application on order management of B2B, we make a standard for the data which will be on the blockchain, based on the standard, we can analyze the data and user access action to mine much more data value.

3.2   Accounting Blockchain

The accounting blockchain solution aims to address the fraud and falsifying of the accounting records. By using the blockchain technologies, especially the irreversible feature, the accounting data can be protected and be surely trusted. We use the proposed architecture to conduct the design of the accounting blockchain system.

Fig. 4. The source tracking of voucher in the accounting blockchain system

Interactions. For the accountant, they use the accounting software to proceed with their works, the mobile and PC client can be considered as the options for their interactions. In real applications, the PC is a frequently-used interaction channel. Particularly, the most popular manner is a SaaS model, we can use this method to provide the online accounting blockchain services for accountant.

Scenarios. Accountants use accounting software to achieve bookkeeping tasks. Multiple tasks about bookkeeping include input the voucher input, set the accounting subjects, set the parameters of accounting. By using the blockchain, two critical tasks can be performed including tracking the source for each book inner the company and triple-entry bookkeeping among companies.

In the accounting system, we develop a source tracking of the voucher, as Fig. 4 demonstrated, the hash value of each voucher is saved into the blockchain, which corresponds to a transaction id in the blockchain network,

Another scenario is triple-entry bookkeeping by blockchain, the accounting party will send the invoice to its transaction counter-party to verify the truth of the transaction. The process is recorded in the blockchain, and the consensus is achieved on the chain. As Fig. 5 shown, the hash address is the digital identity certification by company and individual, which is used as an address to the verifying party of the transaction. The transaction will generate two trusted vouchers for two parties.

Services. The accounting blockchain system is divided into eight services.

1. User management service: the service is closely related to the user, it aims to address the user interaction with the accounting system.
2. Account set management service: it is used to set the configuration data associated with the bookkeeping.
3. Voucher management service: it is used to edit vouchers stored in the database.
4. Book management service: it is used to handle the books generated from the vouchers.
5. Report management service: the service is used to generate the report from the collected books.
6. Block service: this service is to manage chain code (smart contract) deployed in the blockchain network.

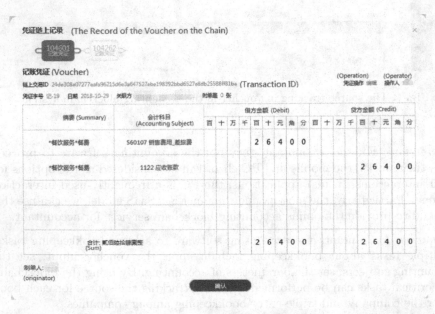

Fig. 5. The triple-entry bookkeeping in an accounting blockchain system

Components. The components of blockchain service are also enabled by Hyperledger fabric, they include three critical parts: permission system, certificate and private key management and triple-entry chain code.

The permission system chain code is used to define the role's permissions in the accounting blockchain system. For diverse users, they have a different permitted range to access the function of blockchain.

The certificate and private key management service is responsible for the private key management of each user. The user will be assigned a certification (X.509) after he finished the registration in the blockchain.

The triple-entry chain code in the accounting blockchain is to realize the business flow of triple-entry bookkeeping on the chain. The chain code can be written by go language supported by Hyperledger fabric tools.

Infrastructure. For the underlying of the accounting block system, we use a cloud based platform to deploy four fabric peers to compose a blockchain network. Moreover, the NoSQL database can be assisted as the business data storage, such as voucher data, report data, etc.

Integration. The service of accounting blockchain allows opening API for other applications or systems. By composing multiple services, such as we compose user management service, account set management service, and voucher management service to form a bookkeeping business.

Data Architecture. The data for the accounting blockchain is divided into two parts. The business data of the accounting system are stored into the NoSQL database, i.e., MongoDB, and the other data saved on the chain are the operation about voucher and report, concretely they are the hash values put into the chain to achieve the source tracking function.

Security and Privacy. To ensure the security of accounting data, we use the permission system to guarantee data permission by different role persons. Meanwhile, we use encryption algorithm AES to protect the vouchers and reports data from leaking for malicious attackers.

Governance. Many interfaces used in the accounting blockchain system. Microservice architecture is employed in the system, we use Docker based to deploy the microservice, all the blockchain services are encapsulated into available microservices for the business of application layer. Kubernates [21] and service mesh [22] are used to conduct the service governance including service registration, service monitoring, load balance, high availability, etc.

4   Conclusion

Based on the proposed open architecture, the developers for blockchain applications can get deep technical insight and guidelines for designing a blockchain solution. The presented BCOA divides the blockchain framework into nine layers. They refer to the design methodology in blockchain related applications. We also use a B2B use case and accounting blockchain case to demonstrate the feasibility and effectiveness of our proposed architecture.

Acknowledgement. This work is partially supported by the Key R&D Program of Guangdong, China (2020B0101090003). This work is also supported by National Key R&D Program of China (2018YFB1402701).

References

1. Zhang, L.J., Zhou, Q.: CCOA: cloud computing open architecture. In: Proceeding of 2009 IEEE International Conference on Web Services, pp. 607–616 (2009)
2. Services Society (2018): Homepage. Accessed 25 Jan 2018. http://www.servicessociety.org/en/introduction.html
3. Nakamoto, S.: Bitcoin: a peer-to-peer electronic cash system (2008). https://bitcoin.org/bitcoin.pdf
4. Etheterum. http://www.ethereum.org/
5. He, S., Ning, Y., Chen, H., Xing, C., Zhang, L.-J.: Layered consensus mechanism in consortium blockchain for enterprise services. In: Joshi, J., Nepal, S., Zhang, Q., Zhang, L.-J. (eds.) ICBC 2019. LNCS, vol. 11521, pp. 49–64. Springer, Cham (2019). https://doi.org/10.1007/978-3-030-23404-1_4
6. He, S., Xing, C., Zhang, L.-J.: A business-oriented schema for blockchain network operation. In: Chen, S., Wang, H., Zhang, L.-J. (eds.) ICBC 2018. LNCS, vol. 10974, pp. 277–284. Springer, Cham (2018). https://doi.org/10.1007/978-3-319-94478-4_21
7. Cachin, C.: Architecture of the hyperledger blockchain fabric. In: Workshop on Distributed Cryptocurrencies and Consensus Ledgers (July 2016)
8. IOTA, IOTA: Internet of Things Without the Blockchain? Bitcoinist.net. https://bitcoinist.com/iota-internet-things-without-blockchain/
9. Zhang, L.-J., Jeckle, M.: The next big thing: web services collaboration. In: Jeckle, M., Zhang, L.-J. (eds.) ICWS-Europe 2003. LNCS, vol. 2853, pp. 1–10. Springer, Heidelberg (2003). https://doi.org/10.1007/978-3-540-39872-1_1
10. Dannen, C.: Introducing Ethereum and Solidity: Foundations of Cryptocurrency and Blockchain Programming for Beginners (2017)
11. Bellare, M., Desai, A., Jokipii, E., Rogaway, P.: A concrete security treatment of symmetric encryption. In: Foundations of Computer Science, 1997. Proceedings., 38th Annual Symposium on, pp. 394–403. IEEE (October 1997)
12. Kovalenko, I.N., Kochubinskii, A.I.: Asymmetric cryptographic algorithms. Cybern. Syst. Anal. **39**(4), 549–554 (2003)
13. Bakhtiari, S., Safavi-Naini, R., Pieprzyk, J.: Cryptographic hash functions: a survey. Centre for Computer Security Research, Department of Computer Science, University of Wollongong, Australie (1995)
14. Krawczyk, H., Canetti, R., Bellare, M.: HMAC: keyed-hashing for message authentication (1997)
15. Hyperledger Fabric. https://www.hyperledger.org/projects/fabric
16. Kosba, A.E., et al.: Hawk: the blockchain model of cryptography and privacy-preserving smart contracts. In: 2016 IEEE Symposium on Security and Privacy (SP), pp. 839–858 (2016)
17. Choon, J.C., Hee Cheon, J.: An identity-based signature from gap Diffie-Hellman groups. In: Desmedt, Y.G. (ed.) PKC 2003. LNCS, vol. 2567, pp. 18–30. Springer, Heidelberg (2003). https://doi.org/10.1007/3-540-36288-6_2
18. EU: Cryptocurrencies and blockchain. http://www.europarl.europa.eu/cmsdata/150761/TAX3%20Study%20on%20cryptocurrencies%20and%20blockchain.pdf

19. US: U.S Congress Officially Supports Blockchain Technology. https://medium. com/@astralcrypto/u-s-congress-officially-supports-blockchain-technology-b5096f097a4f
20. Singapore. http://www.mas.gov.sg/News-and-Publications/Media-Releases/2017/ MAS-cautions-against-investments-in-cryptocurrencies.aspx
21. Kubernates. https://kubernetes.io/
22. Zhou, X., et al.: Delta debugging microservice systems. In: Proceedings of the 33rd ACM/IEEE International Conference on Automated Software Engineering, pp. 802–807. ACM (September 2018)

Author Index

Printed in the United States
by Baker & Taylor Publisher Services